THE TALE BEARERS

The
TALE
BEARERS

Literary Essays

V. S. PRITCHETT

VINTAGE BOOKS
A Division of Random House • New York

First Vintage Books Edition, May 1981
Copyright © 1980 by V.S. Pritchett
All rights reserved under International and Pan-American Copyright
Conventions. Published in the United States by Random House, Inc.,
New York, and simultaneously in Canada by Random House of
Canada Limited, Toronto. Originally published in The United King-
dom by Chatto and Windus Ltd., London, and in the United States
by Random House, Inc., New York, in May 1980.

Library of Congress Cataloging in Publication Data
Pritchett, Victor Sawdon, Sir, 1900-
The tale bearers.
Includes bibliographical references.
1. English literature—History and criticism—
Addresses, essays, lectures. 2. American fiction—
History and criticism—Addresses, essays, lectures.
3. Authors, English—Biography—Address, essays,
lectures. I. Title.
[PR403.P74 1981]   820.9   80-6144
ISBN 0-394-74683-X (pbk.)

Manufactured in the United States of America

FOR MY WIFE

Acknowledgements

The author offers his acknowledgements to the editors of *The New Statesman*, *The New Yorker* and *The New York Review of Books*, in which these essays variously appeared in a slightly different form.

CONTENTS

English

Americans

Characters

7

CONTENTS
Exotics

MAX BEERBOHM

A Dandy

AMONG THE MASKED dandies of Edwardian comedy, Max Beerbohm is the most happily armoured by a deep and almost innocent love of himself as a work of art. As the youngest child of a large and gifted family of real and step-brothers and sisters, he seems to have adroitly decided to be an adult Enigma from the cradle onwards and to be not merely an old man of the world as early as possible, but even to pass as ancient man, possibly on the principle that the last shall be first. If he could not be as tall as his eldest brother, the world-famous actor Beerbohm Tree, he could cultivate the special sparkle and artifices of the diminutive so that one now has the impression that he must have worn a top hat and a swallow-tail coat in his pram. One understands the point of Oscar Wilde's question: he asked a lady whether Max ever took off his face and revealed his mask. Max had no face; or if he did have one it was as *disponible*, as blank as an actor's is. If he had a secret it lay in his quite terrific will and the power to live as if he and the people he saw, were farcical objects.

In his essay on *Dandies* Max Beerbohm asks whether a dandy's clothes can be seen responding to the emotion of the wearer. Needless to say, an instance of this sartorial melancholia is known to him:

I saw with wonder Lord X's linen actually flush for a moment and then turn deadly pale. I looked again and saw that his boots had lost their lustre. Drawing nearer, I saw that grey hairs had begun to show themselves in his raven coat. It was very painful and yet, to me, very gratifying. In the cloakroom, when I went for my own hat and cane, there was the hat with broad brim and (lo!) over its iron-blue surface little furrows had been ploughed by Despair.

'Deadly pale', 'lost their lustre', 'gratifying': only such epithets from a dead usage could release the protest of fantasy that is alive. The art of Max in that passage is shown in a single word: the grey hairs appear 'in' the coat, not 'on' it, as many a comic, careless of the full terror of his effect, would have said.

Beerbohm's detachment must have owed something to the fact that his father came of a distinguished Baltic German family. He had had two English wives: one died, so he married her sister secretly in Switzerland—it was illegal in Great Britain to marry a deceased wife's sister at that time. The father was an amiably slack and cultivated man: the mother engagingly eccentric with a talent for erratic minor alterations in English metaphors. She would say 'I feel as old as *any* hills'— to be old, seemingly, was as important to her as it was to her youngest son. The foreign strain was just the thing to give an edge to Max's talent and that of the family. Expatriation allows one to drop a lot of unwanted moral luggage, lets talent travel lightly and opens it to the histrionic. For his own talents Max Beerbohm could not have chosen a better time. Putting aside, for the moment, such matters as Dandyism, the Aesthetes, the Decadents, the acquaintance of Oscar Wilde, Beardsley, the fading Pre-Raphaelites and the last remorses of the Romantic Agony, no place could have been luckier than London for the wits. The city had many clever newspapers and reviews, the theatre had Shaw and Ibsen to deal with, Pinero and others to insult. It was the time for the fancy of the essayist, for fantasy, the comedy of manners, hoaxes, impersonations, caricature and for carrying on an artist's war with England's fleshly Philistinism, led by a Prince of Wales who looked like a licentious grocer, and for attacking the blustering side of British imperialism, by exaggerating the size of

Kipling's chin and the bushiness of his eyebrows. Max's eyebrows were impeccable question marks. The amount of theatre criticism and essay writing he did as a young man, and the delightful trouble it stirred up among the respectable, is remarkable.

The famous *Defence of Cosmetics* written when Max was still at Oxford, and his closeness to the Wilde and Beardsley set, led some to suspect that Max was on the then dangerous edge of homosexuality. In fact, Max was horrified by the scandalous intimacies of the flesh; his sexual temperature was low— perhaps, as Lord David Cecil suggests in *Max: A Biography*, because he was the last child of elderly parents whose vitality had declined. His temperament was narcissistic—as his innumerable caricatures of himself show—and he seems not even to have attained the narcissism of adolescence, but to have sat with the scrupulous prudence of the demure child in front of any mirror he could find, experimenting in poses and grimaces.

He lived by the eye and—as one can see by his drawings— discreetly beyond touch of hand. Two caretaking wives looked after him in middle and late life and—to all appearances— treated him tenderly if overwhelmingly, as a dangerous toy. And then—how typical this is of an intelligent and sensitive man who is without roots—he turned to literature and the arts for his nationality. Among other things, in the wide-eyed persona he invented, there is sadness. Was it the sadness of not being a genius on the great scale, like his admired Henry James? Possibly. Was it the sadness of knowing that his work must be perfect—as that of minor writers has to be—because fate made him a simulacrum? Or was he simply born sad?

And now to Beerbohm's centenary year in times that are so unsuited to him. Piously Rupert Hart-Davis has done a large catalogue of all Beerbohm's caricatures that have been framed or suitably reproduced, a volume useful to collectors. (It is amusing that Beerbohm's devastating caricatures of Edward

VII and George V, done in his 'black' period, are among the treasures in Windsor Castle.) A selection of essays, *A Peep into the Past*, has also been made by Hart-Davis, and serves to show the development of the essayist. In later essays the charm has become benign and thin, but three of them are excellent: the remarkable spoof portrait of Wilde done when Beerbohm was still an undergraduate and suppressed after the trial, in which occur the well-known lines:

> As I was ushered into the little study, I fancied that I heard the quickly receding *frou-frou* of tweed trousers, but my host I found reclining, hale and hearty, though a little dishevelled upon the sofa.

The other, written on *De Profundis*, denies the comforting view of many English critics of the time that Wilde had undergone a spiritual change after his imprisonment. Beerbohm saw him as still an actor but with a new role.

> Yet lo! he was unchanged. He was still precisely himself. He was still playing with ideas, playing with emotions. 'There is only one thing left for me now,' he writes, 'absolute humility.' And about humility he writes many beautiful and true things. And, doubtless, while he wrote them, he had the sensation of humility. Humble he was not.

And there is the hilarious pretence in another essay that a powerful bad poet of the period—Clement Shorter—had spent his life writing love poems not to a lady but to one of the awful British seaside resorts.

The best American essay on him, in my opinion, was by Edmund Wilson, dry and to the point. There was no mellifluous English nonsense about the 'inimitable' and 'incomparable'. I feared what would happen to Max if he was put through the American academic mangle. There seems to be a convention that this machine must begin by stunning its victim with the obvious, and when I found Mr Felstiner saying, in his study *The Lies of Art*, about the notorious essay on cosmetics that 'Cosmetics were a perfect choice to join the teachings of the moment, aestheticism and decadence,' I understood what Max meant when he said that exhaustive accounts of the period 'would need far less brilliant pens than mine'. But, as I went on, I found Mr Felstiner a thorough, thoughtful, and independent analyst of Max as a caricaturist and parodist. He has good things to say about Beerbohm's phases as an artist in line and water colour, about his absolute reliance on the eye. He is admirable on the parodies in which Max reached the complete fulfilment of his gifts, and his comments on *Zuleika Dobson* are the most searching I have ever read.

Beerbohm caricatured Americans, the working class and the bourgeoisie automatically as part of the impending degradation of civilisation and the arts. . . . John Bull is the crucial figure throughout, shaming himself in Europe, vilely drunk or helpless in the face of British losses, and deeply Philistine. On the evidence of these cartoons, Shaw called Beerbohm 'the most savage Radical caricaturist since Gillray'.

His Prince of Wales is a coarse, tweedy brute, imagining a nunnery is a brothel. His pictures of royalty were savage.

What angered Beerbohm during the Boer War was not Britain's damaged empire—he was indifferent to that: 'the only feeling that our Colonies inspire in me is a determination not to visit them.' It was the self-delusion and debasement of conduct at home, the slavish reliance on grandiose national myths.

But he was no Gillray nor was he a Grosz. He

. . . enjoyed with an eye for what men are individually—for

their conceits, contradictions, deadlocks, excesses. Beerbohm drew more for fun than in the hope of changing attitude or behaviour. In fact he depended as man and artist on the survival of the context he satirised.

Edwardian literature has many, many sad stories, stories whose frivolity half discloses the price a culture is paying for its manners and illusions. *Zuleika Dobson* is one of the funniest and most lyrical and sad of these tales. As in all Beerbohm's fantasies, literary cross references are graceful and malign. Fantasy states what realism will obscure or bungle.

Yet in comparison with previous jocular or sentimental treatments, he could claim to have given 'a truer picture of undergraduate life'. His book points to real elements of conformity and sexual repression. . . . By chance the river itself has the name of Isis, Egypt's greatest goddess, all things to all men. So what emerges is an allegory of Youth forsaking Alma Mater, the Benign Mother, for the consummating love of woman.

Zuleika seems to have been modelled in part on the famous bareback rider whom Swinburne knew, and she has a close connection with 'the Romantic Agony'. She is a 'Volpone of a self-conceit: her mirror is the world', i.e. she is the male dandy's opposite number. Mr Felstiner writes of her rapture when she is spurned by the Duke:

All the world's youth is prostrate with love but she can only love a man who will spurn her. . . . 'I had longed for it, but I had never guessed how wonderfully wonderful it was. It came to me. I shuddered and wavered like a fountain in the wind'— sounds like the joys of flagellation. The Duke even finds himself wanting to 'flay' her with Juvenalian verses. 'He would make Woman (as he called Zuleika) writhe.'

The element of parody insures the tale: Beerbohm's excellence and his safety as an artist are guaranteed because, unfailingly, he is writing literature within literature. Parody, as Mr Felstiner again puts it, is a filter. It drains both literature and life.

Beerbohm rarely drew from photographs. He drew from memory. The recipe for caricature was 'The whole man must be melted down in a crucible and then, from the solution, fashioned anew. Nothing will be lost but no particle will be as it was before'. So Balfour's sloping body becomes impossibly tall and sad in order to convey his 'uneasy Olympian attitudes'. Carson, who prosecuted Wilde, is a long curve like a tense whip, whereas Balfour is a question mark. Beerbohm thickened Kipling's neck and enlarged his jaw to stress the brutality he saw in him. Pinero's eyebrows had to be 'like the skins of some small mammal, just not large enough to be used as mats'. One difficulty, he noted in *How They Undo Me*, is that over the years a subject may change—the arrogant become humble, the generous mean, the slopping scrupulous. Yeats had once seemed like a 'mood in a vacuum' but the youthful aspect changed:

I found it less easy to draw caricatures of him. He seemed to have become subtly less like himself.

As Mr Felstiner adds, a shade unnecessarily,

The truth is that he [Yeats] had become more like himself. . . . An evolving discipline made his themes and his style more tough-minded, idiomatic, accountable.

Mr Felstiner has noticed that in Max's caricatures the eyes of the politicians are generally closed—public life has turned them into blank statues in their own life-time—but the eyes of the writers and artists are open. The eyes of James are wide open—sometimes in dread. Beerbohm wrote a sonnet to him: 'Your fine eyes, blurred like arc lamps in a mist'. Beerbohm's admiration for James and his closeness to his belief in the primacy of art are responsible for the excellence of his well-known parody in *The Christmas Garland*. It required an art equal—if for a moment only—to James's own to get so keenly under the skin; and, like all good things, it was not achieved without great trouble. Indeed, Max added to the famous Christmas story, one more turn of the screw.

He constantly revisited his subjects. His parodies are indeed criticisms and the silent skill with which nonsense is melli-fluously introduced, without seeming to be there, is astonishing. James's manner has often been mimicked, but never with Beerbohm's gift for extending his subject by means of the logic of comedy. I do not share Mr Felstiner's admiration for the Kipling parody: Max was blind to Kipling's imagination though he was daring in suggesting there was something feminine in Kipling's tough masculine worship of obedience. Max here disclosed a violence on his own part. Kipling was as good an actor as he; had been brought up by a pre-Raphaelite father and had as much regard for form and style as Beerbohm had. But, of course, like greater artists, the parodist celebrates his own blindnesses as well as his power to see.

He could even show open schoolboy coarseness in a way that is surprising in one of his circumlocutory habit. There are a few lines on Shaw, an old love-hate, in J. G. Riewald's edition of rhymes and parodies, *Max in Verse*:

> I strove with all, for all were worth my strife,
> Nature I loathed, and next to Nature, Art;
> I chilled both feet on the thin ice of Life,
> It broke and I emit a final fart.

This book has some of Beerbohm's best things: the parody of

Hardy's Dynasts, the pseudo-Shakespeare of Savanarola Brown—only Max could have seen what could be done by splitting iambic pentameters into banal dialogue. The Shropshire Lad is told abruptly to go and drown himself, and for those puzzled about the origins and pronunciations of English place names like Cirencester, there is a gently malicious ballad. Thirty-four of these poems have not been published before, partly because Max was very tactful, at the proper time, about hurting people's feelings—he repressed the keyhole James until after James's death—and partly because he knew when his own juvenile phase had lasted too long.

E. F. BENSON

Fairy Tales

THE EDWARDIAN PERIOD in English literature which runs, I suppose, from the 1880s until 1914 was prolific in light, satirical Society novelists of remarkable urbanity and invention. The exclusive Meredith was one of the gods; the moment for high comedy had come. One can see why: an age of surfeit had arrived. The lives of the upper classes were both enlivened and desiccated by what seems to have been a continuous diet of lobster and champagne—a diet well suited in its after-effects to the stimulation of malice. The class system gave the ironies of snobbery their double edge. Society lived out its fairy-tale life, spent its time changing its extravagant clothes several times a day, and was entertained by the antics of social climbers. And whether they are writing about manners, high, middling, or low, the light novelists have a common quality: they are accomplished, they are even elegant.

For in this static period we must give society a small 's'. Each class felt itself to be exclusive, even the working class. They all stuck up for their manners and practised their own ripe exclusiveness and their peculiar formalities. This is as true of the fashionable like Oscar Wilde, Max Beerbohm, or Saki, who are in and out of drawing rooms all day, as it is of writers of minor classics almost unknown abroad, like the Grossmiths in their *Diary of a Nobody*, or the fairy tales of Wodehouse, the low but polished intrigues of Thames bargees in the tales of W. W. Jacobs, and even the farcical if indigent clerks in Jerome K. Jerome's *Three Men in a Boat*, which was translated into dozens of languages. The worlds of these 'low' writers were as closed, sedate, and as given to their own euphemisms as the fashionable world was: the light novelists survive only if they write well, within their means. I have often thought that professors of English Lit. should take time off from the central glooms of genius and consider these lesser entertainers who are deeply suggestive; but perhaps it is as well that the Academy winces at the idea for we would hate to see our fun damped down by explication.

One of the characteristics common to Edwardian comedy is that it is a fairy tale for adults—indeed in the double meaning of the word. Its characters are seen as sexless. We can put this down to convention rather than to Puritanism, but the artifice does not mean that the novelist does not know or cannot insinuate what is going on under the surface of manners. It may be the point in the *Lucia* comedies of E. F. Benson that his people are neutered and that they are exhilarated and liberated by taking part in a useful psychological fraud. His enormously popular *Lucia* novels, now published in one fat volume, may even be a comically insinuating diagnosis.

What does Lucia, his self-appointed Queen of Riseholme, want as she sits in her fake medieval house or her garden where only Shakespearean flowers are allowed to grow? Certainly not sex. Not even connubial sex; her ruling passions are for power and publicity; she wants the gossip columns to mention her. She wants to dish her rivals. What about her husband, Peppino, writing his privately printed and artily bound little poems? No sex there or, we can guess, elsewhere. The pair have sublimated in dozens of little affectations, their happy marriage consolidated by the lies of baby talk and in snobbish snatches of Italian they have picked up from waiters in Italy. When an Italian singer comes to stay they can't understand a word he says.

And what about Georgie, Lucia's devoted *cicisbeo*, always on the go socially when she commands, playing his bits of Mozart to her, listening to her playing the first movement of 'dear Beethoven's' *Moonlight* Sonata—the second is too fast. Georgie keeps changing his clothes, sits in his doll's house, doing his embroidery, painting a little picture or two, and being 'busy at home' one day a week when he is having his toupee fixed and his hair dyed. Homosexual probably, but no boys in sight; certainly a Narcissus. There is no need to tell us: he gives himself away in his frenzied cult of youth, his fuss about his bibelots, his malicious pleasure in seeing through 'cara' Lucia's snobbery, her frauds, and her lies instantly, enjoying his horror of her as a sister figure he cannot do without. And then there are the various loud masculine ladies of the clique in Riseholme: hearty butches in combat with Lucia's bitcheries; even the surrounding overweight wives with their sulking or choleric husbands are without children and exist in stertorous comic relief. The servants are faithful. The monstrous Lady Ambermere calls hers 'my people,' as if she were an empress. The obsequious tradesmen of the town seem to be the only people engaged—but off the scene—in the vulgar task of begetting their kind.

Since it is not sex that makes this world go round, what does? Gossip above all, spying from windows, plotting about teas and dinner parties, a genteel greed for money and news, and above all matching wits against Lucia's ruthless gifts. Our culture hound, who poses at her window, swots up in the Encyclopedia before distinguished guests arrive, pretending to have read Nietzsche or Theophrastus, can't distinguish between Schumann and Schubert. She steals a guru from Daisy Quantock, hooks a medium—a fake Russian princess—and although these things lead to farcical disaster, she rises above it and is on to the next fad like a hawk. Her dishonesty is spectacular, her vitality endless; and if Riseholme tears her to pieces and is deeply hurt when she inherits a small fortune and takes a house in London to conquer Society there with the same assurance, they long for her to return and, when she does, welcome her with joy. After all, Lucia may have made herself ridiculous but she has come back: she is Life.

Lucia's bids for power in London lead to disasters far beyond the mishaps of Riseholme; but her resilience in intrigue grips us. At the centre of the novels is Georgie—'*Georgino mio*'—and their close relationship is based on fascination—she needs his spite, he needs her deceits. Each is the other's mirror. At one point a delightful opera singer almost snatches him because she can see Lucia as a joke; but this infidelity is nominal. When she shows signs of wanting to be cuddled in Le Touquet, he sheers off in terror and returns to Lucia, forgiven.

We see into the absurd shallows of Lucia's emotional life in two of the central novels in the series. In Riseholme Lucia's social battles are provincial, her artiness is distinctly non-metropolitan, where the medieval revival has become derisively passé and middle class: she had better try to 'keep up'. If she is chasing titled notorieties and Prime Ministers she must drop the Daisy Quantocks who have only just got around to clock golf, and see what smart picture exhibitions, a top gossip writer, or a fashionable divorce case can teach her. The last is a revelation. We see the court scene through her silly mind:

Certainly, Babs Shyton, the lady whose husband wanted to get rid of her, had written very odd letters to Woof-dog, otherwise known as Lord Middlesex, and he to her. . . . But as the trial went on, Lucia found herself growing warm with sympathy for Babs. . . . Both Babs and he [Middlesex], in the extracts from the remarkable correspondence between them which were read out in court, alluded to Colonel Shyton as the S.P., which Babs (amid loud laughter) frankly confessed meant Stinkpot; and Babs had certainly written to Woof-dog to say that she was in bed and very sleepy and cross, but wished that Woof-dog was thumping his tail on the hearthrug. . . . As for the row of crosses [at the end of her letter], she explained frankly that they indicated she was cross. . . . Babs had produced an excellent impression, in fact; she had looked so pretty and had answered so gaily. . . .

As for Woof-dog he was the strong silent Englishman, and when he was asked whether he had ever kissed Babs, replied:

'That's a lie' in such a loud fierce voice that you felt that the jury had better believe him unless they all wanted to be knocked down.

Always a positive thinker, Lucia draws the correct moral: it is no good, it is abhorrent, to take a real lover. Even in marriage her bedroom door is locked and her husband is content. The important thing is to have the *reputation* of having a lover: it gives a woman cachet. In the ensuing folly we see her pursuing a gossip writer who, when he tumbles to her plot, is determined not to be made a fool of like *that*! Gossip writers don't like gossip about themselves; it kills their trade and in any case he is a neuter not unlike '*Georgino mio*'.

Like so many of her enterprises the London venture is a series of disasters from which she recovers fast. Her husband dies of general neglect and a rather despicable inability to keep up with her. She chucks Riseholme and moves to Tilling—which is in fact Henry James's Rye—to deal with a rival more formidable than Daisy Quantock and with lesbians tougher than the Riseholme set. The lady is Miss Mapp, a woman in her forties whose

. . . face was of high vivid colour and corrugated by chronic rage and curiosity; but these vivifying emotions had preserved to her an astonishing activity of mind and body, which fully accounted for [her] comparative adolescence. . . . Anger and the gravest suspicions about everybody had kept her young and on the boil.

As a spy on what is going on she can read the significance in every woman's shopping basket, every window lit or unlit, every motor that passes, what everyone eats, drinks, and

thinks, what every woman has got on, on top and underneath.
Every English village has its Miss Mapp. She intends to be
mayoress of Tilling: Lucia has more hypocrisy and subtlety
and beats her to it. And if admittedly this petticoat war is long
drawn out it does lead to one splendid drama. Tilling (Rye), as
everyone knows, is close to the sea marshes; it is liable to tidal
floods. Miss Mapp is caught trying to steal a recipe in Lucia's
kitchen just as the sea wall carelessly breaks its bank and she
and Lucia are carried into the Channel on an upturned kitchen
table and vanish into the sea fog for several weeks. They are
presumed drowned. There is even a memorial service. Georgie
has erected a cenotaph and a plaque recording their deaths—
Miss Mapp's name is carved in smaller letters than Lucia's!
Of course the two rivals turn up looking very healthy: they
have been rescued by fishermen and have been fed on disgusting cod. Each gives unflattering accounts of the other's
behaviour on the raft and with the seamen, and gives rival
public lectures on the subject. Bitching is the permanent
incentive to Benson's invention and his feline mind.

At the death of Lucia's husband and despite Georgie's total
mistrust of Lucia, he marries her after an enthusiastic agree-
ment that they will never go to bed together. They have that
horror in common. It is noticeable that their affection declines
at once, but their need for each other is increased. Miss Mapp
marries the usual Colonel who, as she knows, is grossly after
her money. But one must not be deceived into thinking that
Benson hates the idiots he is writing about or suffers from
Schadenfreude. Far from it, the sun of comedy shines on his
pages; he adores his victims.

The period is surprisingly the post-1918 one, but that
beastly war is not mentioned. Pockets of Edwardian manners
survived long after that war, for inherited money is the great
preserver of dead cultures. Many of his characters—notably
minor ones like Lady Ambermere, a woman of slowly
enunciated and grandiose rudeness—were in action fifty years

ago. I can remember their accents and their syntax. And here lies part of Benson's absurd spell: his ear for the dialogue of cliques is quick and devastating, for he understands the baby talk of fairyland which, of course, sex and our four-letter words have destroyed. (Unless mass society's own nonstop chatter about 'fucking', 'screwing', and the boys 'having it off' is itself a new fairy-tale jargon.) The minor catchphrases preserve their cracked notes. 'How tarsome!' exclaims Georgie. 'Au reservoir' spreads like measles in place of *'au revoir'*. There is a key to Benson's wicked mind in the following passage between Lucia and *'Georgino mio'*:

> *'I domestichi* are making *salone* ready.'
> *'Molto bene,'* she said.
> 'Everybody's tummin',' said Georgie, varying the cipher.
> 'Me so *nervosa!'* said Lucia. 'Fancy me doing Brunnhilde before singing Brunnhilde. Me can't bear it.'

The key word is 'cipher'. Benson knew the cipher of all his characters. His pleasure was in the idiotic gabble of life. Is he too tepid for export? Years ago Gilbert Seldes compared Benson with the Sinclair Lewis of *Main Street* but pointed out that Lewis spoiled his book by his violent fury. Benson was never furious when he killed an age. He believed that love lasts longest when it is unkind.

RIDER HAGGARD

Still Riding

VERY RARELY, WHEN I was young, do I seem to have had healthy tastes in literature. Mason, Weyman, Buchan, Rider Haggard passed me by. I was afflicted by a morbid interest in the adult and detested those sunny, athletic and strenuous leader-types who are supposed to be the schoolboy's natural heroes. It is only this week, when my duties have obliged me to read Mr Morton Cohen's careful and sympathetic life of Rider Haggard, that I have taken my first plunge into the choking verbiage of *King Solomon's Mines* and *She*, and I am past the age when I can bring to works of this kind the elation of a chaste and hero-worshipping sensibility. What ought to scare me simply makes me laugh. How can people who admire Stevenson, as I do, think anything of *King Solomon's Mines*?

An initiator of the revival of Romance in late Victorian times, his work deliriously received, Rider Haggard never understood why he did not rank with Stevenson, Meredith, Henry James and, shall we add?, Falkner, the author of *Moonfleet*, Kipling, who was his great friend, or Joseph Conrad. Today he would find his place among the gaudier historical or horror films or among the new school of science fiction writers. Like many popular best-sellers, he was a very sad and solemn man who took himself too seriously and his art not seriously enough. The fact is that he was a phenomenon before he was a novelist: other novelists are content to be simply themselves, Rider Haggard was his public.

To be identified with the public is the divine gift of the best-sellers in popular Romance and, no doubt, in popular realism. E. M. Forster once spoke of the novelist sending down a bucket into the unconscious; the author of *She* installed a suction pump. He drained the whole reservoir of the public's secret desires. Critics speak of the reader suspending unbelief; the best-seller knows better; man is a believing animal. So, in the age of religious doubt, Rider Haggard tapped the mystical hankerings after reincarnation, immortality, eternal youth, psychic phenomena. He tracked down priestesses and gods. So, in a peaceful age, he drew on preoccupations with slaughter; and, in an empire-building age, on fantasies of absolute, spiritual rule in secret cities. His triumph—though it baffled him—was in the creation of *She*. The journey into mysterious Kor comes flawlessly out of the agonies of sexual anxiety; Ayesha herself is an identifiable myth or rather a clutter of myths: everything from Jung's Anima, the White Goddess, *la belle dame sans merci*, down to the New Woman or, as Henley said, 'the heroic Barmaid, the Waitress in Apotheosis'.

But the remarkable visions of Rider Haggard would have got him nowhere without three other qualities. One of these cannot be praised enough: he is a constantly inventive story-teller. The other two, paradoxically, support it: his stories are so tall that only bad grammar and slipshod and even vulgar writing can get him round the difficulty; and he dare not go in for more than pasteboard character. Anything in the nature of a human being would stand in the way. Look at Stevenson and one sees the enormous difference. Finally, Haggard has the enviable gift (common to many writers of popular Romance) of pouring it all out in a great gush in a few weeks. He has the confessional form of genius. He never corrected a line.

Rider Haggard was one of the sons of an explosive and eccentric Norfolk squire who was feared by his family and 'awful to his tenantry'. The boy was backward and considered to be such a fool that he was given a poorer education than his brothers had had. He was subject to extreme fears. He was devoted for years to a doll. One of the odd traits that remained with him all his life, was a childish mannerism of speech. He pronounced his 'r's' as 'w's' and always said 'v' for 'th'. A phrase like 'a very thorough rogue' (Mr Cohen says) would become 'a vewy fowough wogue'. But if he was the fool of the family, the family had a firm sense of its social privileges. The Squire got the youth on to Bulwer's staff when he was sent out to be Governor of Natal.

The experience transformed him. In a very short time, emancipation from his father, the shock of Africa and a taste of responsibility, woke up the sleeping mind. He had arrived at the birth of an empire. It was he who 'planted the flag' in the Transvaal; it was he who worked with those who were putting order into the ramshackle legal system of the Boers. Above all he admired the Zulus and got to know them intimately. He hunted, he travelled and explored, and he listened to legends. He must certainly have heard of Zimbabwe, the prehistoric city of stone; and although later he denied that he had heard tales of the white woman ruler of the Lovedu tribe in the Transvaal, he travelled close to their country and the customs of the Lovedu closely resemble Ayesha's Armahaggers.

By this time Haggard had become a collector both of facts and of objects, a habit that led him, later on in life, to write an excellent documentary work on rural England. It also led him to turn his house in Norfolk into a grotesque and oppressive African museum. This collecting habit has an important bearing on his visions: they are a sort of dramatized ragbag. Nothing impresses so much—if we are spiritually at sea—as the spiritual furniture depository; it protects us from the pain of selecting and deciding. In Haggard's time, collecting offered the pleasures of colonizing spiritually; his antiquarianism was a religion in itself.

Haggard's mind was almost totally serious. His humour, always uncertain, is clumsy and vulgar. Midway in his African adventure, he received an emotional shock from which he did not perhaps care to recover. He was jilted by a beautiful girl.

She may have owed something to this disaster. And when he returned to England and married again and, tragically, was to lose his son, one notices that Haggard is one of those men who harden over and do not recover from blows. Still later on in life he became explosive and irritable. The Haggards had loud voices; they were said in Norfolk to be able to 'chat across a field'. It is not a bad description of his manner as a novelist. He wrote to be heard a long way off.

So the impression one has is of a tall, handsome, bearded, wounded egotist, unable to stand criticism of any kind, who carries his secret sorrows rather histrionically. The tough man with the sorrow about which he will not speak, is his characteristic narrator; and, once more, one recalls how much the creative impulse of the best-sellers depends upon self-pity. It is an emotion of great dramatic potential. He had a good deal of pride and he accepted its burdens. The result of the enormous success of the booby of the family was that he had to rescue his brothers or their families from the financial messes they had got into. They did not demean themselves by showing much gratitude for the extraordinary generosity of the man who had been dismissed by his father as 'a greengrocer' and a contemptible 'penny-a-liner'.

The blood lust and the moralizings are the worst things in the Haggard novels; the dramatic invention—the old witch crushed by the closing stone door in the cave, the sight of the mummified explorer in *King Solomon's Mines*—is marvellous and so also is the first vision of the mountains, although in description he is usually better in local detail than in the set-piece. The sunbeam that lights the plank when Ayesha, Leo and the narrator are crossing the precipice in *She* is a brilliant stroke; and the account of the sinking of the dhow and the ride through the breakers in the same book is admirable. A collector in everything, Haggard had the art of piling it on. It is an art. His flow is molten, burning from one event to the next. And although we have to stress the triumphantly naïve part played by his unconscious we have to repeat that he was a voracious and intelligent observer. His two serious works, on English farming and the political issues in Africa, show him to be capable of the serious historical document. On one plane, the very great writers and the popular romancers of the lower order always meet. They use all of themselves, helplessly, unselectively. They are above the primness and good taste of declining to give themselves away.

Mr Cohen has many interesting critical comments on Haggard's work and especially on the celebrated problem of the significance of 'She-who-must-be-obeyed' and of the journey through swamps and down tunnels into Kor and the mystic presence. He follows the hint of Mario Praz and thinks Ayesha to be the type of exotic *femme fatale* who appears in Victorian literature with the decline of the hero: the heartless beauty, pitiless, cold, a close relation of Wilde's Salome—or Henley's terrifying barmaid. She is, in Haggard's account, more male than female: I am inclined to call her *He* but—as James Thurber once said about a grand piano—with breasts.

Ayesha is undoubtedly a disturbing figure and, I think, because she is a compendium. Soon after the book was published Haggard added to the confusion of her character by comments of his own. It is his misfortune that his compelling imagination could create a creature of primitive and over-mastering passion and savage jealousy and yet, at the same time, apply the most trite Victorian moralizations to her case:

> I saw him struggle—I saw him even turn to fly: but her eyes drew him more strongly than iron bands, and the magic of her beauty and concentrated will and passion entered into him and overpowered him—ay, even there in the presence of the body of the woman who had loved him well enough to die for him. It sounds horrible and wicked enough, but he should not be too greatly blamed, and be sure his sins will find him out.

And there is a curious suggestion, somewhat coarsely made, that if the love of the temptress is evil, many men have found respectable marriage to be hell. Haggard's rhetoric sounds like the kind that is clumsily covering up.

One is led to speculate on the inner life of a generation that responded eagerly to his allegory, to the fantasies of masochistic travel, to those precipitous mountain walls, those caverns, tunnels, caves and tombs, and all the bloodshed. And who liked to have it all dressed up in prose that is at one moment all baccy and Norfolk tweed and, the next, Liberace's trousers. Yet his African books represent a real response by a most suggestible man to African legend, which—as we have seen recently in the works of Amos Tutuola—is far bloodier than anything Haggard put down.

Mr Morton Cohen indeed argues that his books may find a place in an African, as distinct from an English, tradition. He compares Haggard with Fennimore Cooper, pointing out the distinction that Haggard was writing for a people with a future. 'When they assert their independence and rule once more in their native lands Haggard's Zulu saga may come into its own. For he captures in it a clear, engaging picture of Zulu life and comes to terms with the turbulent Zulu spirit.' He is writing especially of *Nada the Lily*. I have not read it but if in that work he completely freed himself of Norfolk, then I can see that the speculation is an interesting one. He had in his impure imagination something powerfully accessible.

RUDYARD KIPLING

A Pre-Raphaelite's Son

The Strange Ride of Rudyard Kipling—the title of Angus Wilson's long-awaited exploration of Kipling's life and works is well chosen by an author who himself is a novelist, a searching critic, and an intelligent traveller who knows India and has his own early 'colonial' connection with South Africa. Kipling's 'ride' was indeed an exotic one, not only because of a childhood and youth passed between India and England, his sojourns in the United States, South Africa, and, later on, his habit of wintering in Cape Town and in France; but because of the restlessness of his eye and temper. As with many Victorian Englishmen change whistled by in his ears, his mind was the explorer's: in his middle years it also opened outposts in history, in Roman Britain and Christian Antioch, but also in his clinical studies of illness—illness itself being an inexorable country we are bound to know: its scenery was psychosomatic. Like many of the colonizing kind he became more gaudily English than the English in the sense that Englishness became an extra conscience and a personal cause. That cause was Kim's, whose passionate cry 'Who is Kim?' indicates Kipling's similar search for an identity within a caste.

The main outline of Kipling's ride has been established with authority by Charles Carrington, and Angus Wilson acknowledges that debt. He has elaborated the story in lively detail by his own researches, interviews, an exhaustive reading of the works, and his own speculations. The result is a very full and clever book. It shows Kipling as he grows and changes through the phases of his life—Wilson really does succeed in the always difficult task of domesticating the man in the circumstances

31

and fantasies of his daily life and times. If the manner is personal and diffuse, and the narrative circuitous as it moves forward and then goes back to reconsider, this is the habit of a gifted and serious talker. Mr Wilson is outspoken when he finds Kipling dropping into vulgarity, sentimentality, over-dramatizing, or covering up; yet he confesses to a sneaking feeling for Kipling's philistinism even when he is most fervent in his admiration for the artist and craftsman. He puts Kipling's imperial afflatus in historical perspective, as he deplores the novelist's sneers at 'the long-haired liberal intellectuals'. Kipling was a hero-worshipper of men of action, especially common soldiers; but he could not match them.

His lasting attraction as a writer is his gift of conveying the magical. It springs from his childhood in Bombay and Lahore, and he never lost it entirely. Even the offensive belief in the supremacy of the white race is a form of projected moral magic, a boyish fantasy perverted by an adult. Kipling worshipped children, and easily and seriously abandoned himself to their private minds. For him, as Wilson says, children create a vast world of magical explorations within a small space as they make their maps of 'hazards and delights'. He saw childhood as the sacred age out of which it was painful and shocking to grow: until he was sent back from India to school in England, his own was blissful. The visual quality of Kipling's prose is not photographic but a perpetuation of the clarity and unquestioning response of the child's eye; it was this that gave him his unmatched sense of surfaces and place.

He had also the child's ear, the ear for magic in language, and it rarely turned into adult whimsy. In one of the Mowgli stories—which he wrote long after he had left India—the man-cub has to repeat 'the Master Words of the Jungle' he has learned from Baloo. 'Master-words for which People?' the seven-year-old Mowgli asks, delighted to show off his good memory of bear-talk, bird-talk, snake-talk. And boasts that one day he will have a tribe of his own. 'Now you have nothing to fear,' says Baloo. 'Except your own tribe,' mutters the panther under his breath. (We note that Mowgli has had these languages knocked into him by the clouts and blows, called 'love pats', from the panther. The boy deserves them because he is impertinent and swanks: he feels a sensual pleasure in the pains of discipline.)

There is much of Kipling as a man and writer in that talk from the fable of 'Kaa's Hunting'. He spoke Hindi before he spoke English; and the English he inherited was strongly marked by the Biblical cadences he had drawn from his Ulster Scottish and Yorkshire Methodist forebears, preachers uttering their didactic magic, softened though it was by the Pre-Raphaelite tone of his cultivated parents. He became the chameleon-like multilinguist who could enter the talk of common soldiers, engineers, workmen, and the Sussex peasants, or the rhetoric of the public speaker, changing his colour as he became for the moment one of them. The gift sprang from what he called his daemon—a very Pre-Raphaelite word—and the daemon was harnessed to Wesley's 'gospel of work'.

Here Mr Wilson raises a matter that will develop later on. Kipling had little interest in his own ancestry, which may seem strange in one 'for whom piety toward the past of mankind, whether historic or pre-historic, and toward his own childhood', was strong, but Wilson does not think this had anything to do with his dislike of a narrow religion. He writes:

To lay emphasis upon personal heredity would be at once to assert the personal aspect of a man's identity rather than the group heredities of nation, race, caste and place which are man's true strengths and loyalties, and to lessen, by leaning upon genetic determination, a man's reliance upon himself, his absolute accountability. . . .

When we ask why Kipling's sensitive father and intelligent if possessive mother sent him 'home' to England at the age of six with his three-year-old sister, to live for years with the awful family of 'Baa, Baa, Black Sheep', the Nonconformist belief in self-reliance and accountability must have played its part, though the Kiplings' own Methodist beliefs had lapsed. The Victorians had strong reason to believe that the Indian climate was dangerous to children: Mrs Kipling had just lost a baby when the children were sent off. And there was common talk of the precocious sexual habits of Indians—racial fears are commonly rooted in sexual obsession. Mr Wilson adds the important note that to be able to afford to send one's children back to England was also a sign of social status: the clever Mrs Kipling was out to push her shy husband's career. At 'The House of Desolation' in Southsea Captain Holloway and his wife seemed respectable: the captain was indeed a decent man and his wife's ferocious manner and Calvinism were not detected.

With his usual sympathy Mr Wilson does his best to be fair to Mrs Holloway and brings out more fully than any other account of the episode that I have read the real nature of the drama there. The Holloways were typical of that common Victorian category: the genteel family with the anxieties of people going downhill—poor relations. Mrs Holloway was jealous of young Kipling who was better connected than her own son and encouraged her son's bullying; and, like so many children sent home from overseas, the young Kipling was a swank, defiant and rebellious. In short the boy had to adjust himself to a new jungle—the English.

At this time his eyesight began to fail and his terrors doubled. Already he was a child who lived by sweeping metaphorical images, and he spoke of the dark coming into his head. And the dark, as Mr Wilson says, was suggested not only by failing eyesight and the violent punishment from Mrs Holloway but by his first experiences of death: his baby brother had died and presently the kind Captain Holloway dropped dead: the one mollifying influence at Southsea had gone.

Angus Wilson rejects Edmund Wilson's judgement on the lasting influence of the 'Baa, Baa, Black Sheep' experience as being schematic psychologically, and indeed I agree that Edmund Wilson's political hatred of imperialism distorted what was elsewhere a penetrating essay in *The Wound and the Bow*. The influence of Kipling's schooling at Westward Ho seems to me more important. Once again, the parents made a choice that looked good and was within their means. Westward Ho was a minor public school which would not put the rubber stamp of the great English public schools on the gifted boy; but it was not the roughhouse of *Stalky & Co*. As so often happens in England the place flourished as an anomaly: intended to train boys for empire-building and the military life, it was run by a progressive crank and intellectual who shared the artistic tastes of the Pre-Raphaelites. His house was full of Rossetti drawings; he was devoted to William Morris and was even radical in politics; he was deep in English, French, and Russian literature. (In the school debating society he proposed the resolution that 'The advance of the Russians in Central Asia was not hostile to British power'. The young Kipling opposed it and got the militant schoolboy chauvinists to defeat it.)

Although Kipling was badly bullied in his first year, the perceptive headmaster allowed him the run of his excellent library. He soon spoke and read French rapidly and even tried Russian for a while; he read Pushkin and—above all—Lermontov, whose laconic manner made a lasting impression on him: all odd experiences in an empire-builder's school. As for the bullying, as we know from *Stalky & Co.*, he soon had his own élite gang or tribe, who were clever at running the traditional schoolboy secret society, outmanoeuvring the bullies and inventing the schoolboy guerrilla practice of cunning and crude practical jokes. Kipling never lost his taste for boring practical jokes as a comic form of vengeance: the story 'Dayspring Mishandled' is essentially this. The nasty thing was the cool and sadistic bullying of the 'baddies' by the 'goodies', who learned to take pleasure in the pain of others. This is common enough in human nature, but it has too much crude relish in some of Kipling's stories and (as in contemporary films of violence) has deplorable moral overtones which attract the philistine public. Kipling survived Westward Ho: his physical incapacity for games was an advantage and it also increased his double regard for duty relieved by cunning. Another point Mr Wilson makes is that at small country colleges boys succeeded easily in going out of bounds illegally among the people of the countryside. The place offered something of the day school's closer relation to everyday life outside.

Kipling is one more of those English novelists who did not go to the university. That might have taught him to think, but he was not by nature a thinker, he was an image maker. Not much is known about his night prowling in the London streets. Nor is enough known about his prowlings in Lahore when he returned to be a newspaper reporter at the age of seventeen, beyond what can be guessed from his stories. What, the modern biographer asks, was his part in the sexual half-world of London or India? He clearly observed it. Did he participate? No one knows, but one would guess that, at the last moment, a romantic with a strong imagination acting within a stoical discipline would not have done. There is more 'magic' in sin if it is not committed. Stories like 'Without Benefit of Clergy' may make us doubt; but Kipling was a born watcher and listener. He certainly opposed the closing of brothels to English troops, but that was because he took the part of the lonely British soldiers whom he knew well. His early, mild love affairs sound painfully platonic; and he was certainly mother's dutiful boy and continued to be so in his marriage. The most important experience in the rootless or gypsy part of his early life, Angus Wilson thinks, occurred when he went up to Peshawar and on to the no-man's land of Kabul:

From this border ride, Kipling's imagination must have carried remote and terrible sounds.... The horrors came to him, I think, from the *visual* scene of the passes....

Here, at last, he was in the region talked of in Lahore bazaars, the lawless, treacherous land whence came Mahbub Ali, the horse-dealer, a real live disreputable acquaintance (as well as the ambiguous fictional protector of Kim). Here in an atmosphere of intrigue and vengeance, or power preserved by a brutal, irrevocable jesting justice like that of our Tudor Age, he found a terrible version of Stalkyism. Where the rough and ready practical joke may put things right in the simple, harsh world of boarding schools, torture and prolonged death agonies are authority's jest in Afghanistan where the slightest threat to the throne may shatter all rule and let loose tribal anarchy. From the bazaars of Peshawar and from talk with those in the Amir's entourage upon this 1885 assignment come, I think, the cruel teasing death of the blind mullah in 'The Head of the District,' and the deathly joke of 'The Amir's Homily,' and at least two powerful neglected poems— 'The Ballad of the King's Mercy' (1889) and 'The Ballad of the King's Jest' (1890). From these we see that those who suffer terrible punishment are not the open enemies of authority, but those who seek to please the King too much, or talk too much, or carry out too easily his cruel commands, or over-flatter him.

Angus Wilson believes that Kipling's stature rests on his fictional India, not only on *Kim* and the *Jungle Books*, but on *Naulakha*, *The Barrack Room Ballads*, and his Indian short stories. After he left India in 1889 he returned only once for a short time two years later. He had political squabbles with his paper and the authorities, but above all, it was under his mother's prompting that he left for fame in England and in

America. There was an immense gain for the depth cf his skills but, Mr Wilson thinks, at a cost to his poetic imagination. There is indeed a split and an increase in strains and tensions as the master craftsman takes over, as resourceful in his crude popular work as in the best of his compressed and intricate stories: it is a split which has some connection with being torn between his 'riding' life and his belief in the family square.

Mr Wilson's book is remarkable for its brief or extended comments on pretty well all the Kipling stories as he threads them through the life, and he thinks that modern critics over-value the late stories, which are compressed psychological or emblematic dramas; he believes the present taste for the late Kipling arises out of literary fashion and our boredom with India. I differ, to some extent, from Kipling's biographer and critic here. Kipling was hostile to Congress and the changing Indian situation. He was an artist whose India stops with the idyll of *Kim*. He was incapable of writing a novel, even on an English theme; his mastery would inevitably appear in the short story—a form which depends on intensifying the subject, stamping a climate on it, getting at the essence of it.

As they grow older, short story writers tend to repeat themselves as Maupassant or Maugham did; Kipling escaped this by his variety and his boldness with usually intractable subjects and by increasing his difficulties. This last was well-suited to lifting the lid on his personal conflicts. I am with Mr Wilson in thinking that the terrifying story of 'Mary Postgate' is probably one of the finest stories in our language and becomes all the more impressive in our own terrible times. But I find 'Dayspring Mishandled' intolerably obscure and mannered, despite its apparent compassion. I think Mr Wilson has missed the significance of 'Mrs Bathurst', in which a rough lot of seamen and railway workers in Africa evoke the memory of a kindly woman who ran a bar they all knew and who came—it is suspected—to a ghastly end, seemingly with a lover no one can identify. Mr Wilson complains that Kipling never brings this woman on the scene and gives no clue to the identity of those cindered bodies on the railway line. It is, I agree, maddening not to be told. But the story is marvellously placed; Kipling is a master, even in his single-narrator stories, of making his narrator seem to be neighboured by other voices. In 'Mrs Bathurst' the several talkers are contributing from what they half know and half feel. They don't really know exactly what happened, but what they are revealing is themselves, and, in the end, what looks like a collective guilt—to what Mrs Bathurst of their own have they reasons to feel guilt and a horror of inexplicable fate?

The story stirs a collective fantasy which has its roots in some memory in their crude and inexpressive lives. Mrs Bathurst was apparently a decent woman but she was much more the *vision* of a decent woman. What have these men done in their time to a decent woman? A story which might have been one of sentimental remorse or a revelation of one disgusting man's sin, or even of her weakness, strikes a blow at each of them, all the more savage because it is gratuitous. That heap of cinders on the track is the common agglutination of a death—and Kipling feared death.

If we look at the change of note and intention in the voice, line by line, in the opening passages of 'Love-o'-Women', we see how fast he can announce a drama and intensify it line by line:

> The horror, the confusion, and the separation of the murderer from his comrades were all over before I came. There remained only on the barrack-square the blood of man calling from the ground. The hot sun had dried it to a dusky gold-beater-skin film, cracked lozenge-wise by the heat; and as the wind rose each lozenge, rising a little, curled up at the edges as if it were a dumb tongue. Then a heavier gust blew all away down wind in grains of dark coloured dust. It was too hot to stand in the sunshine before breakfast. The men were all in barracks talking the matter over. A knot of soldiers'

wives stood by one of the entrances to the married quarters, while inside a woman shrieked and raved with wicked filthy words.

The passage has sometimes been criticized because it is mannered; but line by line, it reveals his strange congregation of words. There is the classic desire to be as spare and drastic as a ballad, the temptation to sail off into what one imagines Henry Irving was like when he declaimed 'The Bells'. There is that unbearably exact photograph of drying blood—the lozenge. And then the aesthete's glance at the ancient craft of goldbeating, which—if one has ever watched goldbeating— precisely conveys the Biblical message that all flesh enters the process of becoming dust. In the last sentences, Kipling achieves his decisive and characteristic effect; he roots the story not in the 'I' or 'me' of the narrator but in 'our' common experience. Kipling's characters are always thickly neighboured: the story exists in the minds of all who were there.

The comments on these particular stories come in the middle of the book and are an example of Angus Wilson's disconcerting leaps out of chronology. Back to life then, and to the questions that have to be asked. The quarrel in Vermont was an unlucky family row with relations, perhaps stirred up by Kipling's half-American wife. There was a good deal of the severe French bourgeoise in her. Kipling was hot-headed, bursting with Britishness, and she lacked tact: Brattleboro thought the pair were snobs. Up until then he had loved America, except for the violence and the American dislike of privacy—an old trouble between Americans and the British.

The odd thing is that his scapegrace brother-in-law, who was at the heart of the ridiculous trouble, was just the kind of character Kipling was more than half drawn to. But in his Vermont period he was naïvely amazed that Americans were cold about his suggestion of a Pax Anglo-Saxonica. The notion was muddled: it was essentially the ambiguous imperial creed, just as 'Recessional' is one of the hymns that can be sung in two voices, the patriotic or the repentant religious warning against bragging. Both voices, Mr Wilson says acutely, were surely addressed to himself; he knew that he must not be carried away by his popular skills; if he bragged, the powers of his daemon would depart. He was a very superstitious man:

> Of course, Kipling meant every word of his Imperial beliefs and gave most of his surface active life to them, but I am sure that the excess of the tensions they produced, his political frenzy in the years 1900–1914, can only be fully understood if one grasps that his fear of anarchy or foreign tyranny, his hopes of a sane, ordered Pax Britannica, a Pax Anglo-Saxonica, or, at last, a Pax Franco-Britannica were also a reflection of the deep inner struggle between the anarchic, romantic childlike force of his creative impulse and the ordered, complex, at times almost self-defeating pressure of the craft he imposed upon it.

On the question of Kipling's marriage and particularly on the criticisms of the character and behaviour of his formidable wife Carrie, Mr Wilson is very fair. She was certainly very domineering—and like many dominant people was liable to hysteria which her prisoner was called upon to calm. She was certainly, once more, a stern mother-figure. He was incompetent with money. She managed his financial affairs, his contracts, his correspondence. She is said to have opened all his letters and to have dictated the replies. Her daughter said she cut her husband off from stimulating intellectual company and indeed she was out of her depth in it. But she fiercely protected his privacy and stood between him and the plague of visitors who descend like vultures on famous men; if Kipling *was* cut off from his coevals, he was cut off chiefly by his wealth: his friends were the successful and important. She was suspicious by nature, particularly of women, and seems to have felt many people were really after his money. But Kipling appeared to enjoy her rule, for he had been used to an excessive reliance on his parents, even in middle life. Visitors noticed that Rudyard and his Carrie shared the same harsh jokes.

She probably enjoyed hearing that the female of the species was more deadly than the male. Possibly he would not have married her *unless* he had loved her charming brother first and more spontaneously—he responded most to family affection—and one must remember that he and Carrie had the tragic bond of the loss of their two children and that she nursed her misogynist through his serious breakdowns and his hysterical, baseless, but harrowing dread of cancer. No; brought up in a tough school, Kipling found a tough wife. As for his restlessness—rich and comfortable, the pair who hated the English winter spent five months of the year abroad, especially in France, which he loved.

What is Mr Wilson's final judgement on him?

He was a gentle-violent man, a man of depressions and hilarity, holding his despairs in with an almost superhuman stoicism. Manic-depressive does no more than repeat this in big words. I prefer if I must a socio-historical description of long generations of Evangelical belief ending in post-Darwinian doubt.

He feared to know himself, but

[the critic] has to say that this persistent evasion of introspection, of further questioning of the source of the despair and anxiety and guilt that enmesh so many of his best characters in his best stories, does keep him out of the very first class of writing. . . . *Kim*, I believe, is great in its own right; and, for the rest, he did so many, many things very well indeed that the greatest novelists never saw to do.

JOSEPH CONRAD

A Moralist of Exile

TO THE EMINENT father-figures—Galsworthy, Edward
Garnett, Wells—who were in fact uncle-figures, as we shall
see, and who nursed and praised him through the years when
the great public ignored him, Joseph Conrad had the magne-
tism of a shaman risen from the ocean. In London literary
circles he passed as the mysterious Romantic Slav—all the go
at that time—a typical misrepresentation; there was nothing of
the Russian *exalté* and deplorable Dostoevsky about him, as he
firmly pointed out. Surely the British had realized that the
Poles despised 'the Russian soul' and were Westerners to a man.
Flatteringly he had gone through the British mill and become a
British master mariner, had even read Marryat when he was a
boy; it had been noticed that he was a shade stand-offish on the
decks of clippers and avoided the crew when ashore. In a very
thick and explosive accent, he would talk about Pater and
Flaubert to the rare officer who had literary tastes.

These mischievous Edwardian impressions have their charm;
once the ironic disparagement of Bloomsbury and Cambridge
had passed by in the Thirties, later generations have understood that Conrad's genius was not merely descriptive; he was
one of the great moralists of exile. And exile is not emigration,
expatriation, etc., etc., but an imposing Destiny. He was
marginal, even a drifter 'with prospects', until well into his
thirties. In the course of an exhaustive psychological study of
Conrad's three distinctive lives as a Pole, a British seaman,
and a novelist, Professor Karl says:

Conrad found in marginality itself a way of life, a form of

43

existence, and a philosophy that added up to more than survival and well-being. In probing exile, dislocation of time and
place, language disorientation, and shifting loyalties, he
extended our view of the shadows of existence. Indeed, he
suggested that the shadows were to be the main area of existence in the twentieth century.

So long as we do not take this to mean that Conrad was an
early Existentialist or Outsider Professor Karl's words are
acceptable. Marginality has its own tradition: Conrad thought
of himself as a kind of Ulysses, when he was young. When one
or two Polish critics accused Conrad of 'betraying' his country
by leaving it to write in a foreign tongue—'for money' one of
them ludicrously said—they were as foolish as those who
attack Henry James, T. S. Eliot, Joyce, Beckett and Auden for
expatriation. The 'ground' to which the exile naturally belongs
is bilingual, trilingual, language—not simply as syntax but as
image, metaphor, and even conceit. A certain passivity and
perhaps circulatory in-turnings of imagination may be the
interesting price.

The last substantial biography of Conrad was done by
Jocelyn Baines in 1961 and was discerning in a formal chronological way. Baines had a good deal to say about Conrad's
Polish background; since that time a large number of unknown
letters have come to light, and in the course of editing these
Professor Karl has put together a richer Life that aims to get as
close as possible to the complex interweaving of the novelist's
real life and temperament as they were drawn into his work.
Karl's ideal biography is George D. Painter's life of Proust,
chiefly because he sees Proust and Conrad preoccupied with
the imaginative retrieval of memory. He has sought to fit
Conrad into Henry James's half-mocking sense of human
experience. As James put it,

Experience is never limited, and it is never complete; it's an
immense sensibility, a kind of huge spider's web of the silken

threads suspended in the chambers of consciousness and catching every airborne particle in its issue. It is the very atmosphere of the mind.

In consequence Professor Karl is a circuitous narrator, following Conrad's psychological threads back and forth. The reader may be maddened but must be patient as he treads and retreads old paths. For example: Conrad's so-called 'duel', which was really an attempt at suicide in Marseilles when he was twenty, is re-examined three times in sixty-two pages, but only in the last account does Professor Karl tell us what almost certainly happened and why, pointing out that there is an inordinate number of suicides in the works. Such a circling about incident is of course very Conradian; how long we have to wait when we read *Lord Jim* before we are allowed to know *what* the trial of Tuan Jim is about. So *Lord Jim* is to be thought of as almost completely an intrigue of memory—but in a double sense. The ostensible trouble we recognize at once:

Based on an actual event, the entire novel is structured on various commentators recalling what occurred, or trying to make sense out of what has become for them part of a distant now dim past.

The other 'memory' spreads into guessing: *Lord Jim* and its ship the *Patna* are not simply a paradigm of Conrad's feelings about Poland 'but the expressions of material lying deep within him'.

The very country into which Conrad was born created divisiveness and was based as much on memory as on contemporary life. . . . It was not only the country into which he was born that required constant artifice, it was the family also. Conrad's immediate family was itself split between idealistic and practical elements, with personal tragedy at its base and gloom, morbidity, and self-destructive obsessions as its routine experience.

The argument is interesting, though Professor Karl's prose does run into uneven patches. He hangs some heavy platitudinous quotations from other scholars on Henry James's slender spider's web. Since I have nothing but admiration for Professor Karl's command of the living detail necessary for an exhaustive biography of 1,000 pages, I hate to see him making solemn and obsequious gestures to the academy. Writing of Conrad's life as a seaman he drags in some words of Erik Erikson:

> Those twenty years at sea were not at all a waste but fell into what Erik Erikson, in a somewhat different context [i.e., writing of Gandhi], was to call the *epigenetic principle*. As he explains it, it is a principle derived from the uterine growth of an organism, although Erikson's use of it indicates that 'anything that grows has a ground plan, and that out of this ground plan the parts arise, each part having its time of special ascendancy, until all parts have arisen to form a functioning whole.'

Bully for the estimable Erikson. But we do not need Erikson or Gandhi to remind us that, in the case of Conrad,

> the sea years conditioned [him] to the disproportion of sea and land, to differing perspectives of time and space, and to the kind of tedious staring that becomes inertness and passivity in his work.

Conrad was doubly an exile, even before he left Poland at the age of seventeen: his country did not belong to him; it was not independent. It was divided between Russian and Austrian rule. Conrad's father, Apollo Korzeniowski, was of the gentry, a wildly improvident, gifted young man and a natural Don Quixote and plotter. The mother's family, the Bobrowskis, belonged to the stern Catholic aristocracy with large estates who had their rebellious past, but out of aristocractic self-interest had become accommodating to Russian rule and confined themselves to keeping what they held.

Both families had a deep contempt for commerce, though Conrad's uncle on his mother's side was a rationalist conservative who said that commerce at least had a moderating influence on Utopian ignorance of economic reality. Not so Apollo; two years after the Polish insurrection of 1861 he was still plotting. He was arrested and sent into exile with his wife and child. Their health was destroyed: the mother's sufferings brought her to an early death when the child was seven; the father was overcome with grief and remorse, turned mystical, and died when the boy was eleven. We see the child following his father's coffin through the streets of Cracow at a funeral that became an unforgettable political demonstration.

The romantic cause of Polish freedom had decimated both sides of Conrad's family: he had become dramatically orphaned. He had lost not only his parents but the influence of the ideology they represented. He was stranded in a spiritual wilderness. Some biographers have drawn a pitiable portrait of an ailing little boy who was thought to be epileptic and liable to become consumptive, sitting in silent misery with an extravagantly solitary and religious father, and stunned by the experience. Professor Karl rejects this view. In the first place the boy responded to his father's gifts as a distinguished poet, playwright, and translator: he was drawn to Shakespeare, Dickens, and, above all, Hugo's *Travailleurs de la Mer*, a book that must have had a powerful influence on Conrad's desire to travel or to go to sea.

In these influences Apollo was a really rewarding father, but in his political disaster and his Quixotism he represented the failure of faith, the loss of belief in solid ground. It was noted that the parentless boy would tend to run wild, to resemble his headstrong father and dream of escape and adventure; and that ne would use his bad health and neurasthenia as weapons for getting his way. Far from being pitiable, the child became formidably difficult, recalcitrant in learning, obstinately determined to get out of his impossible, futureless country. He did get away—but as Professor Karl shows he took the dilemma of his relations with his loved and yet deplored father with him. It is Professor Karl's habit to shoot forward to the novels that twenty years ahead would still show Conrad struggling with the dilemma his father had left him in. In *Victory* we see the exploration of

> the most intimate of father-son relationships in [Conrad's] work; in the interplay between Axel and the older Heyst ... he noted the ironic ambiguities of the relationship: portraying the father as if he were Apollo *after* his fall [i.e., after the insurrection], who, having finally seen the futility of all action, cautions silence, cunning, and withdrawal. . . . By turning the relation into an ironic and a paradoxical one, Conrad relived the situation.

A surrogate father was, in fact, Conrad's salvation—up to a point: his mother's brother, Uncle Tadeusz Bobrowski, a wealthy and lonely widower who became the boy's guardian. Tadeusz was everything Apollo had not been: he became almost as much a mother as a father to the boy whose inherited recklessness was to plague him for years.

> Tadeusz Bobrowski was himself a man of many sides. . . . As well as being a somewhat narrow moralist and positivist, he was a person of considerable intelligence and insight. He has unjustly been described as a right-wing conservative, even a reactionary force, thrusting upon Conrad a rationalistic, legalistic approach to life and its goals. Although some of this is correct—and should not be denied—Tadeusz deeply resented the Nałęcz [i.e., Apollo] strain of foolhardiness and self-destruction. . . . He represented elements of balance and sanity.

In the correspondence with his nephew, which went on until Conrad's thirties, Tadeusz is a harassed and sometimes deceived Polonius advising the careless Laertes. He leaned toward the new scientific ideas but without much faith in the technological mind and certainly without optimism. (That would be a bond with his nephew, as was also his enormous reading in many languages.) It is an important point that Conrad's often reactionary views on politics and society did not outgrow his uncle's and those of his uncle's class: he certainly stuck to his uncle's hatred of revolution:

> We can assume that part of Conrad's withdrawal from the full political implications of his novels, or his caution in dealing with such matters, derives from lessons learned from Bobrowski: that the individual who joins movements, thinks politically, or tries rapid reform throws himself under the wheels of the juggernaut. Evolution, not revolution, [Mr Karl leaps forward to *Under Western Eyes*] Razumov warns. Gradualism, for Bobrowski, was the sole hope, but even that modicum of optimism would not be acceptable to Conrad the writer.

Conrad came to believe that 'the individual intensifies his essential being and rides it to his doom,' pitting himself against an absolute and implacable destiny. We recall, Karl says, Stein's injunction in *Lord Jim*: 'to immerse oneself in the destructive element'—an Apollo–like utterance, except that Stein adds, as Uncle Tadeusz may have done—'and by the exertions of your hands and feet in the water, make the deep sea keep you up'.

The sea! We come back to the youth who, having read *Les Travailleurs de la Mer*, nags his uncle to let him become a seaman. One of the refractory devices becomes commoner: a skilful, perhaps hysterical use of bad health which eventually marked the whole of his life. (It is true that gout, rheumatism, and arthritis caught most seamen sooner or later.) But bad health gives freedom—freedom to read immensely, to avoid education and discipline. A large number of young men all over Europe who hated commercial society opted for the sea, travel, and adventure. The ports were crowded with them; there was a slump in shipping. For Conrad the sea would be a beneficent wilderness, above all for one who found he preferred the staring loneliness of the watch and the undoubted appeal of the beauties and terrors of fatalism. (Conrad also uttered some of his rhetorical words about the sea being a mother, delightful to Freudians, but a thoroughly second-rate generality, in an artist: I fear Mr Karl thinks it mythically 'significant'.)

Conrad was better when he spoke of the sea as a mirror. He had been staring at maps, longing to be tested by a new country. So Uncle Tadeusz gave in and let him go to France, the second home of gifted Polish émigrés, and, on a pleasant allowance, the young gentleman hung around in the port of Marseilles—a period he would late in life romanticize in *The Arrow of Gold*. One has the impression of Conrad being very much a dandy and poseur in his youth, perhaps inclined to play the aristocrat and man of honour, reckless with his money, sending home for more, and very Apollo-ish as a young wit and intellectual, playing at being Ulysses. Then comes the mysterious crisis: there are few berths on French ships, a lot of hanging about, angry letters from uncle, an urgent debt, and then, inviting the man who was his uncle's watchdog to tea, Conrad shoots himself, fortunately missing his heart: he will always overact. The French dream is over, a possible French novelist is done for—perhaps for the simple reason that the British merchant service had overwhelming prestige; more likely that the British were slack and unscrupulous and did not ask many questions; perhaps because he wanted to enter the new wilderness of a speech which he did not know, but whose literature he knew very well.

Professor Karl would like to think that Conrad had picked

up some knowledge of the Symbolists in Marseilles. An attractive idea, but there is, he agrees, no evidence. The conjecture is pleasant and would be fitting. Really, Shakespeare and Dickens were more important, for they also brought with them a way of accepting the literary enthusiasms of a father whose political and philosophical life he rejected. To write in Polish would have meant the duplication of his father's disaster. His choice of the English language and métier amounted to a divorce. English also got him out of the landlocked Mediterranean and out to the East, to the casualties of colonial competition and exploitation, to the monstrous scandal of the Congo and the greed in *Nostromo*. It is strange and moving to see Conrad struggling with his own restlessness, submitting to discipline, trying to escape it, always secretive, not quite certain of what he is hoarding but hoarding because as a visionary artist he will need an immense amount of vivid detail to draw on.

Professor Karl is excellent on Conrad's strange marriage to a stoical but vocal girl of humble London family who had to struggle for a living, and though she was out of her depth intellectually, Conrad was devoted to her. Perhaps there are glances at her depressing background in *The Secret Agent*: Galsworthy admired her and she certainly stood up to Ford Madox Ford.

During twenty years at sea Conrad had been a misogynist with a sailor's deep mistrust of women: the captain who takes his wife to sea is done for. The crew can't bear it. The only woman who seems to have matched Conrad intellectually was his novel-writing 'Aunt' in Brussels, but he eventually drifted away from all attachments once he had got what he wanted— which was not sex but moral support. The *femmes fatales* of his novels are the standard fantasies of the Romantic Decadents. Once he had settled in England as a storyteller his life was a hell of toil, muddle, the instant recognition of his talent by a few, his total rejection by the great public. They preferred the gaudier Kipling or Haggard to the morbid and elegant Pole, who thought of art as the transcendent reconciling illusion— like the sea, a mirror.

From his letters and from his conversation one would gather that Conrad was one of the most tormented of novelists whose agonies, blockages, and misfortunes can only be compared with Dostoevsky's. His health was wrecked by the time he reached his fifties; the *contretemps* of family life appeared to him as apocalyptic disasters. He was extravagant and was always in money difficulties which paralysed him. He became strangely commercial with collectors of his manuscripts.

It is odd that a novelist who had his enormous, vivid experience to draw on should have been stuck so often with nothing to say. Edward Garnett believed that he lacked invention. Memory, unless it is involuntary, is indeed static. As an expatriate Conrad was unable to draw on a body of experience common to his prospective readers. It is interesting to know that so much of his background material and so many of the episodes in his novels were suggested by reading, but, of course, the great novelists often owe their decisive power to their ability to turn their incapacities into qualities. If invention flagged, Conrad intensified his static scenes. When the realistic advancing of character beat him, he invented the garrulous and rather too clubbable Marlow as a narrator who could jump ahead; if a character did not move, Conrad used great ingenuity in labouring the character's moral uniqueness.

His people are morally and physically stamped like medallions, and he himself referred to his desire for an effect of sculpture. At his greatest he indeed achieved a sort of condensing and dramatic authority in vibrant and living stone; his seascapes are more alive than many of his people. He is careful to take his characters out of time into an isolated world very much in the manner of the dramatist—the ship, the small obsessional enclaves of conspiracy, the unget-at-able port in *Nostromo*, the captain's cabin in *The Secret Sharer*—so that the utmost can be got out of the closed moral dilemma. He was not among the great creators of character. He was an establisher of fates and situations. He wrote:

> I have been called a writer of the sea, of the tropics, a descriptive writer, a romantic writer—and also a realist. But as a matter of fact all my concern has been with the 'ideal' value of things, events, and people. That and nothing else.

The world of ideal values becomes, so often, the exile's island in a world which has become doomed because he has no country. The connivance of Conrad's sense of these values with his own sense of isolation and catastrophe made him one of the most searching psychologists of that moral conflict in the European novel.

T. E. LAWRENCE

The Aesthete in War

LOOKING BACK ON T. E. Lawrence and his legend after forty years one sees in him exactly the Hero called for by those who fought in the First World War and survived. It is perfect that he went into that war as the romantic happy warrior and emerged as the guilty Hamlet of his generation. In a far less theatrical way, so did others who fared worse: whatever singularity or genius *they* had was ground out of them on the Western Front where the 'real' war was being fought.

To them—and to the public trying to forget that mass slaughter—Lawrence's guerrilla war in the desert was war as they romantically dreamed it ought to be: terrible, but at least apprehensible like an exotic work of art, small yet visionary and having the epic quality of individual combat—known then only to flying men—in which the daring young leader leaps to privilege, gets his freedom to act alone, and wins by his courage and his cunning. And, as if this were not enough to dream of, the hero has the gift of enlarging his own legend so that it continues as he renounces his victory and abases himself. What, after forty years, has overtaken him? The Partisans and Resistance leaders, the guerrillas and underground fighters of the Second World War and after, have made clear that, at any rate, T. E. Lawrence was a sketch for a coming prototype. Or the reviver of an ancient one.

If heroes fulfil the unconscious wishes of others, their rank depends not only on a *virtu* that springs from their internal conflicts and their vision, but on their historical opportunity. Lawrence without British imperialism in its penultimate phase behind him would have had no driving force. Even the duplicity that haunts political visionaries would have failed him. And one cannot throw out the fact that, in mass societies like Britain and the United States, fame is made glamorous by the commercialized press and films, and by the hero's talent for staging himself and even for acting out the exceptional man's natural disgust with success. None of the reviewers of *Revolt in the Desert* (the abridgment of *The Seven Pillars of Wisdom*), Lawrence wrote, has 'given me the credit for being a bag of tricks . . .' and he added with some vanity, 'too rich and full for them to control'. Inevitably the denigrators took the tip and looked into Lawrence's powers of mystification. The most extravagant in malice was Malcolm Muggeridge:

> [Lawrence] is superlatively the case of everything being true except the facts. Who more fitting to be a Hero of Our Time than this, our English Genet, our Sodomite-Saint with Lowell Thomas for his Sartre and Alec Guinness to say 'Amen'.

Bringing all the shallowness of the debunker and the meanness of the disappointed man, Richard Aldington added T. E. Lawrence to his 'exposures' of D. H. Lawrence and Norman Douglas. The most charitable comment one can make of Muggeridge and Aldington is that they were attacking the image created by the popular press and the films and ridding themselves of the postwar spleen at T. E. Lawrence's expense: he had tried to do it, more painfully, at his own.

But there *is* an obvious difficulty for biographers in dealing with Lawrence which John E. Mack points out in his long study *A Prince of Our Disorder*; the excellent title is a phrase of Irving Howe's. Dr Mack first approached the subject of the making and self-making of a hero as a psychologist but found himself in regions beyond the clinical. Dr Mack is no wit. He is a very repetitive writer; he has loaded and lengthened his book with worried platitudes. Lawrence, who was debonair and clear even when he was evasive in his own remarkable *Letters*, puts his own case better. Still, Dr Mack is thorough. He has searched and interviewed widely and feels even personal sympathy with his intractable subject. He says two things which are fundamental. The first could be more tersely expressed by saying that T. E. Lawrence was Irish in his taste for fantasy, as Shaw well understood:

> One of the purposes in writing [*The Seven Pillars of Wisdom*] was to invite the public to create with him a new and different self, a mythological Lawrence, larger than life, a self that would be immune to or beyond personal pain and conflict and that would replace the self he felt he had debased. . . . The irony is that, objectively, the real Lawrence corresponded in many ways to the ideal one he sought to create through his dramatising and embroidering. But from his inner psychological perspective that real self was debased by the war.

The second point is certainly exact whether one looks at Lawrence's upbringing, his education, above all at his prose style, or at the war and his career afterwards. He was a good deal the aesthete in war.

> Lawrence is in many ways a transitional hero standing . . . between the neo-medieval romantic heroes of the nineteenth century and the moral realists of the twentieth.

If not a Hero, he exemplified what happened at a breaking point of European culture in 1914.

Lawrence's private story is the story of the wound and the bow. He had by birth the distinction (which passes as a fantasy through many children's heads for a time) of being illegitimate. His mother also had been an illegitimate child, the daughter of a journeyman shipwright in Durham, and farmed out on sternly religious Scottish families. She was sent at eighteen as a nurse to Ireland to look after the children of an unhappily married, hard-drinking, Anglo-Irish landowner called Chapman who passed his time hunting, shooting and fishing. They fell in love, he left his wife, changed his name and went to Wales, then to the south coast of England for the sailing and finally, since their four boys needed a good cheap secondary school, to Oxford. The new family had £300 a year left to live on, a respectable if modest private income in those days and representing the protective assurance of capital.

The two parents were devoted, the landowner accepted his decline in status and relative poverty happily: it could not have occurred to him to earn his living. He was by inheritance a rentier. The young Scots girl, of course, soon dominated him. She stopped him drinking and was the figure of power in their little villa. They were a deeply religious couple, an odd but determined pair of Puritans who disapproved of theatres, dances and shut themselves off from the curiosity of neighbours. Perhaps they were too discreet, for Lawrence senior went off at times to Ireland to see his sporting friends and to keep an eye on his estate: in Oxford a land agent would inexplicably arrive. It was not long before the Lawrence boys guessed the secret and although the indirect private effect on them was crucial, they benefited by their parents' serious care for their education: the secondary schools they were sent to had special opportunities for getting clever boys into Oxford.

The boys were stamped by the mother's Puritan religion in which, Dr Mack thinks, she evidently saw as her redemption for the sin of taking a man away from his wife. I find this too simple; her religiosity was an assertion of pride. Lawrence's mother had charm and he inherited her strange, vacant, yet penetrating china-blue eyes and undoubtedly her will, which was powerful to a degree. She was a fanatical housekeeper, all for cleansing house, body and soul: the prudent austerity is common to Calvinist Scotland, northern England and indeed

Germany and is far more the expression of superior virtue than of guilt. She did believe in discipline and physical punishment. She was determined to break the will of her mischievous second son by beating him on the backside and initiated him into the sensations of pleasure-pain: it is easy to argue that the mother (who was a remorseless questioner) was very conscious of her own guilt; if so she was close to being a Justified Sinner. This did not prevent her from enjoying the vanity of the humbly born in having carried off her grand landowner, in Lawrence's own words, as 'a trophy'.

The Victorians had resources in the subtleties of the class system: the one thing that must have protected the Lawrences was that the elder Lawrence was recognizably a gentleman; not only his self-effacing manner but the public respect for his mysterious private means guaranteed the view. But what was his influence? He was devalued, but on the mind and imagination of T. E. Lawrence his influence was enormous. The Anglo-Irish gentry were colonists who had been either Elizabethan or Cromwellian conquerors, soldiers all of them, rewarded with captured estates. They intermarried mainly with their kind and became tied up in hundreds of years of cousinage. It was a near enough assertion that one of the elder Lawrence's ancestors was closely related to Raleigh and, it was even claimed, he had Raleigh's looks. But the strongest element in the family was Cromwellian Roundhead and Dutch: it dulled the Elizabethan dash and brought in the Low Church Puritanism of Anglo-Ireland. The race traditionally bred soldiers but by the nineteenth century the soldiers, rakish or sedate, had become dull landlords who did little but talk correctly of horses, salmon, and snipe, though their brighter sons occasionally became Britain's best generals or outstanding servants of the Empire.

What Lawrence senior embodied for his famous son was a sense of history as an inheritance. What the self-isolated family of brothers gave to him was a lasting belief in the exclusive superiority of self-sufficient extroverted masculinity and brotherhood. This and the mother's power over her sons was enough to ensure—as Dr Mack suggests—Lawrence's chastity. He had no adolescence: he went straight from boyhood to manhood. It was part of the mother's plan of redemption that one at least of her boys should be a missionary in China: sexual purity was essential, marriage an obscenity.

The well-known avidity of the young Lawrence's studies in archaeology, his passion for medieval castles, the history of chivalry and the Crusades, and his curiosity about the Saracens were the perfect preparation for the desert war and the vision of Arab freedom. He was teaching and hardening himself. Like Doughty and other educated Englishmen who went as solitaries to the desert, he felt the pull of tribal life and the masculine cult of personal honour, long ago lost to Western life. (Honour and its concomitant knowledge of treachery had a battered meaning for the Anglo-Irish, and were perhaps a survival of Elizabethan influence, especially Raleigh's.) When Feisal discreetly showed that he had guessed Lawrence was doctoring the telegrams from Mecca and said dryly: 'You always prefer my honour to your own', the words have the accent of an Elizabethan conceit, the ambiguity of words cut by the diamond of a betrayed Tudor on his window. Anti-imperialist, as Lawrence was, he was drawn to the military fascination of Imperial power. Oil was commerce and therefore contemptible, but Alexandretta must be 'held at all costs'.

In his political and military account of the war Dr Mack's eye is on Lawrence living an acquired legend. All has the fire of gifted youth until we get to the crises—what really happened when he was captured at Dera'a and what Dr Mack regards as the vengeance or the loss of self-control at the Turkish massacre of Tafas: here a hidden Lawrence appears. Which of the several versions in the re-writing of the rape at

Dera'a is to be relied on? Is it, conceivably, a fantasy to cover some other act of sodomy? Research by Lawrence's sceptical or believing critics is not conclusive, as Dr Mack shows, but he is confident that an act of sodomy did occur and is certain there was a brutal beating; Lawrence's revisions are an attempt to tell the truth that shocked him, though 'the sequence of events is hard to follow'. There was an assault, Dr Mack concludes, 'and the element of sexual pleasure he experienced in the midst of such indignity, pain and degradation was particularly intolerable and shameful to him'. It has since become known that when Lawrence tried to hide in the ranks of the RAF after the Peace Conference and was in despair he hired a man to beat him brutally from time to time and concocted a grotesque fiction that would persuade a simple man to do it.

The difficulty of the biographer and especially one with wide—that is to say not simply clinical—psychological interests lies in avoiding the static summary of hindsight and showing a man as he changes. Here Dr Mack is good in portraiture and plausible in analysis. Lawrence's nature and his sexuality were not formed by a single cause. He was a mixture of the craftsman and aesthete in war. The literary tastes of his generation were very much directed by the Victorian cult of the medieval, a self-conversion to a heroic past which would disguise the defilement of the industrial revolution; the imaginations of the educated were filled with Chaucer, Malory, William Morris, Tennyson's *Idylls*, Jean Froissart, the *chansons de geste* and the ethic of courtly love. William Morris and Doughty wrote in a studiously mannered prose, so did Kipling the popular novelist.

This imagination was Lawrence's—he admitted to 'doing up small packets of words foppishly'. He swung between plain direct words and the imagery of masquerade. In the Twenties one finds him admiring Cabell's very dubious pseudo-medieval *Jurgen*, which is enough to show the split in his own mind. The rarefying, unsexing and idealizing of women was borrowed from the neo-Romantics and the abhorrence of fleshly contact confirmed the message. Strangely this suited well with the demands of Empire which required men who could stand being alone and could live by self-discipline. Lawrence's mother would enter such a conspiracy without necessarily being driven by guilt: she would be asserting a faith and the fortifying of conscience. And one can add that sexual aberration is well known to be common among explorers and men of action who are fanatical, as Lawrence was, in hardening themselves to endure punishment.

Like pretty well all the men who came out of the 1914 war Lawrence had a badly damaged mind. At All Souls he was either sunk in deep depression or would suddenly tell wildly imaginary stories of his exploits. He both sought and hid from publicity. The visionary at the Peace Conference had the angers of an actor who is now in a political play he does not understand or rather understands too well. He hated the betrayal. He was forced to accept the moral consequences of the double role he had played in Arabia. Dr Mack writes of the exits and entrances in the drama frankly, though he is not writing as an historian. Shaw, who understood Lawrence as a fellow Irishman and who was an expert in what Lawrence called 'the solution of multiple personalities', told him that the limelight would follow him for the rest of his life; and one cannot say that Lawrence avoided it—at least not for many years.

The 'self-degradation' was dramatic as an act of conscience and punishment, even staged, yet clearly a genuine attempt to come to terms with himself. The RAF was a hard school, the Tank Corps was bestial. One has to read *The Mint* to see what he willed himself to go through. Most biographers, as I have said, have thought he inherited this will from his ruling mother, and yet in his exposed detachment one also sees the image of his father. The old landowner (who had become a baronet and had died by this time) must himself have been something of a spectator in his own family when in his time he had given up his status and, in the course of 'lawless' passion, had joined the common people. The fates of father and son have curious resemblances. We also have the not uncommon sight of passionate elders using up a family's erotic capital, leaving the children with little or none.

Lawrence was a Don Quixote before he became a Hamlet. What remains for us of the former? He was one of the first to see that after 1917 Asia itself was going to be a political force, even if he tried to see the Arabs as part of the then British Commonwealth—the imperial idea of Lionel Curtis. He imagined a natural coming together of the Jews and Arabs, too simply because he could not foretell what new imperialism might intervene. Arab commentators think he judged the situation badly. As Hamlet, he saw his career in the desert as a prostitution: his introspections, as Dr Mack shows, do reveal how 'unlovely the back of a commander's mind must be'. I do not think he was playing with conscience in the pedantic Irish way: he had his mother's earnestness.

How does his service in the ranks of the RAF and Tank Corps now strike us? Here he is tragically vivid in Dr Mack's portrait. The poor devil would slip out of the depôt at night and was pitied by the sentries whom he silently passed. The service was intended as a therapy, but he was forced to live among common men who had become unwanted animals because they could not get other jobs: what most upset him, characteristically, was their obsessive lust. They were quite different from the conscripts of World War II who were politically-minded and, whether educated or uneducated, shared far more the common lot of a whole population. The therapy, if there was one, was public and not private. I think that Dr Mack's strongest compliment is that Lawrence was a born 'enabler'. He was a natural technician, a practical craftsman and teacher; he could get on with anybody and help people to help themselves. But his private philosophy of renunciation and a 'decent nihilism' did not save him from a deep boredom. Driving fast and dangerously on a motor bike to 'forget himself for a few minutes' was an escape into nihilist sensation. Not a suicide but a loss of will.

E. M. FORSTER

The Private Voice

IT HAS OFTEN been said that the British venerate old age. The sins of the ancient are forgiven for they have become 'characters'—a national ideal. Even the talented survive their inevitable denigration: they have freed themselves from the national obsessions with social obligation and the virtue of worry. This is true of E. M. Forster who lived until he was ninety and who had become a kind of wayward holy man by the time he was seventy: a status he would hardly have achieved in France, for example, where old age is often publicly derided. Perhaps the British cult is simply Victorian, for the Victorians solemnly sought to get over youth as quickly as possible and assume elderly airs—children died like flies—and here one must note that the famous liberal, humanist, rationalist intellectuals seem to have had a gift for longevity. One can argue, of course, that they were all born whimsical and elderly; this was sometimes the impression given by Forster who was elderly when he was a boy and in many ways schoolboyish to look at when he was old: the tweed cap too small, the sleeves of the shabby jacket too short, the shoes neglected as he skipped across to King's College chapel at Cambridge to hear the Sunday singing. He looked like a whim.

More decisive suggestions appear in Mr Furbank's biography which, while not ignoring Forster as the psychological and social 'case' or strange 'instance' he certainly was, re-creates him and his succeeding circles of friends in close chronological detail and illuminates the intimate life that ran, often underground, with his public career as a novelist, critic, essayist, and figure of controversy. So much critical work has been done about him that it is a relief to see the man himself. He was at once comically drab and alarmingly alive, and so fresh in the offhand private voice speaking in the public place where it disconcerted because it dodged conventional utterance. The voice was the most important thing about him and his prose; it was unofficial, conversational, free of jargon, and dropped a dissident but carefully timed word or two of Edwardian slang into the solemn moments of argument. One or two of these malign words stick in the mind: certain kinds of thought and action did not 'pay'; or about his own kind of merit in which he liked to be that problematical racehorse, a possible 'cert'.

Mr Furbank's *Life* is long perhaps for a writer whose abstentions were long, but Forster's life was filled by seminal friendships with the eminent in literature, politics, the universities, and high administration; with Maharajahs, coolies, busmen, barbers, policemen, casuals, and soldiers and—it strikes one—perhaps the largest collection of female relatives any famous writer has ever had. The oddity is that this range of aunts, cousins, and connections came to a man who was shy and even timid, and yet drastic in moral courage, kind but tart when irritated, and who to many seemed old-maidish. Mr Furbank, a friend of a much younger generation, does not standardize his subject as a psychological case: he watches him live with perceptiveness and sympathy. He simply shows that Forster's dilemmas are deeply entangled with the privileges and manners of the class into which he was born, with emotional fatality and the rewards of a slow self-discovery.

There is so much detail in this book that the reviewer has to skip many piquant things. In 1879 when he was born, an only child, Forster was the odd product of interlocking families of the prolific and very mixed Victorian middle class. The important ladies came variously from the rich banking Evangelicals, known as the Clapham sect, who had in the past been eminent in the antislavery movement and had followed the traditions of philanthropical Puritanism and liberalism.

From Northumberland appear clerics who became Anglo-Irish and, in the course of generations, returned to Britain to comfortable livings—Forster thought he owed his independence and his imaginative gifts to the Irish and also a Welsh connection. Another strain was from a penniless, rather Bohemian family once distinguished in marine painting who ended as modest teachers with occasional hushed-up scandals and embarrassing connections with 'trade'. There was present also a County connection led by a huntin' and shootin' uncle who was terrifying at the dinner table (his favourite battlefield), who had genially savage ideas about 'making a man' of his nephew and whose attitude to religion was 'If the house is religious, wear your trousers out and pray like blazes.' The uncle was exceptional.

But by 1879 Forster's relatives had become mainly part of the tame and snobbish semi-suburban class of independent means. They might be called the watered-down and villa-dwelling successors of the people in Jane Austen's novels, formidable at tea, but without the iron of the eighteenth century or the raffishness of the Regency in them. The working class and the poor were 'unthinkable'. Soon after Forster was born his young father died of consumption; a grandmother and aunts flocked to the rescue of the young mother who was proper, lively, capable, but in narrow circumstances. A duel was fought over the baby who was expected to be as frail as his father had been; he was therefore cosseted and spoiled and turned into a passionate and imperious child, a girlish mother's boy who played with dolls and was made precocious by adult company.

The inner 'sureness', the adult air Forster carried throughout his life, was established for good; but he was not being equipped to survive the horseplay and bullying and the gang life of English boys at private schools. They were quick to spot a 'muff'. E.M. were bad initials—he was very soon called 'Emmy'. A more serious and central situation developed

between mother and son: they adored each other. He wanted
to marry her, of course; and that delightful phase did not
quickly fade. She refused—it is believed—to remarry because
she doted on him, and his love for her embraced his long life.
(She died when she was ninety and he was sixty-six and for a
great deal of the time they occupied the same houses.) The
hearty huntin' and shootin' uncle—and other uncles—complained of the boy's stumbling helplessness and incompetence—
he couldn't even carry a tea tray without dropping it—and
could see no future for him.

And then, there was the taboo subject of sex. When he was
sent, rather late, to his first prep school, schoolboy smut
puzzled him: at home his penis was known as his 'dirty' and he
thought of it as some kind of punishment; well, children do
perhaps still stick to peculiar ideas, but this one lasted. (In later
life he said that it was not until he was thirty, and after he had
written three distinguished novels about love and marriage,
that he understood how sexual intercourse took place.)

But a sinister initiation into sexual practice was experienced
when he was eleven years old. While walking on the Downs
he fell in with a middle-aged gentleman in a deerstalker hat
and knickerbockers who had stopped to have a pee. The man
asked the boy to play with his penis. The young Forster was
startled by the man's fierce-looking organ but politely did as
he was told and was astonished by the result. The man also
offered him a shilling which he refused. The boy ran back,
frightened, to school and at once wrote home to his mother
about it. She made him report the incident to a master at
school, which he did. He was miserably embarrassed, the
schoolmaster was inept. By now the boy was in a 'hard and
important mood', enjoying the limelight there and at the local
police station. He said boldly the man could easily be identified
because his organ was 'diseased'. The curious thing is that he
had before all this told his mother about the 'dirty trick' of
masturbating. He was naïvely surprised by her distress and he

decided he would never be frank again. 'So ended,' he said, 'my last chance of a confidant.' If he couldn't talk to the adored mother, to whom on earth could he ever talk?

Mr Furbank suggests that if the incident was forgotten it left a lasting pattern of panic and cross-purposes and that perhaps he returned to it in *Passage to India* where it became a model for Adela's vengeful and confused behaviour after she imagines she has been molested by Aziz. By his mid-teens Forster was no longer the imperious spoiled darling; he was a despised 'day boy' at Tonbridge School—the hellish Sawston of *The Longest Journey*—an enemy of the Public School regard for leadership and the team spirit. He was already a prim, buttoned-up, and pedantic intellectual, widely read, demure, and a sharp judge of the character and snobberies of Tonbridge society. One or two clever boys thought he was certain to enter the Church and become a bishop. He left school and, since his father had been an architect, he was taken by his mother on a tour of French cathedrals in France, the first of many continental journeys with her in the next years.

After the French cathedrals, freedom. A beloved great-aunt made a substantial trust on his behalf which would make him independent for life and in 1897 at the age of eighteen he went up to King's College, Cambridge. He was, Mr Furbank points out, no awestruck provincial: he would never have mistaken the famous gateway for medieval. If he fell in love with Cambridge, it would not be in the tragic fashion of those who were content to live ever afterward a scholar-gypsy life:

> For good or evil Cambridge gave a special stamp to the careers [of the sons of the professional middle classes], prolonging boy-hood and opening fresh vistas—of friendship, of intellectual self-fulfilment, of social climbing—at an age when for most of their contemporaries the choices had been made. . . . Cambridge cushioned his existence ever afterwards.

There he started the process of 'finding himself'—a process which emotionally was to take an excessively long time, largely because of the possessiveness of his mother.

The main thing about Cambridge for him was that it was the place where things were valued for what they were in themselves and not for what use you could make of them. He was there in the G. E. Moore period and although, in Mr Furbank's view, too much has been made of Moore's influence (Forster never read *Principia Ethica*), the epigraph stuck in his mind as the 'idea of Cambridge "truth": "Everything is what it is, and not another thing".'

The received ideas of Tonbridge vanished. Forster cut a dim figure at first but he had influential friends in the enormously assured Darwin family. In his fourth year he was intellectually fit to be elected to the 'secret' society of the Apostles which after eighty sleepy years had woken up. Their arguments about 'states of mind' and 'what exactly do you mean?' bored him. ('Arguments,' he once said, showing that he was a novelist by nature, 'are only fascinating when they are of the nature of gestures and illustrate the people who produce them.') The university also confirmed in him a prejudice which had been established in Britain early in the nineteenth century. It is one which still haunts British life and was an aspect of liberal thought: the prejudice that the scholars, civil servants, and the professional classes were the successors of the landed aristocracy and were the people who ran Britain—not the businessmen, or indeed their workers, who merely made the country rich. It is a theme which, in his sternly self-critical way, Forster dramatized in *Howards End*.

The Apostles who in 1901 exacted honesty in their debates spoke out about the taboo subject of homosexuality. Furbank thinks that by this time Forster must have known that his upbringing had made him homosexual by temperament. The 'love-affair' with his mother must have ruled out any possible attraction to other women. And

It would seem likely that, partly as a result of the traumatic experience at his prep school, the onset of puberty had brought with it very strong sexual inhibitions—so much so, that for much of his youth and early manhood, physical sex played very little part in his conscious thoughts; he did not have much in the way of erotic fantasies, or, if he did, they were infantile ones.

Even when he succeeded in breaking through his inhibitions, Forster does seem to have been a man of low temperature sexually. The homosexual affections he felt at Cambridge were platonic. The aftermath of the Oscar Wilde trial made gossip about homosexual practices secretive. Mr Furbank gives this portrait of him at the time when he had struck Lytton Strachey as being 'a taupe' [i.e. a mole]:

he was drab-coloured and unobtrusive and came up in odd places and unexpected circles. There was something flitting and discontinuous about him; one minute you were talking with him intimately, the next he had withdrawn or simply disappeared. He was freakish and demure, yet at times could be earnestly direct, as if vast issues hung upon simple truth-telling. And all the time there was something hapless or silly-simple about him; friends likened him to Henry VI. . . . Yet there was a queer sureness about him, a super-quick sensing of immediate situations, and—in flashes—an extraordinary sweep of human understanding.

In the next ten years Forster lived the decorous life of the intellectual with his mother in their suburban villa. He had no particular career in mind, but he had begun to write. He satisfied his social conscience by teaching Latin in the well-known Working Man's College in Bloomsbury where many distinguished men had given their time, and he worried about the cultural snobbery of autodidacts like the Leonard Basts of pre-1914 Britain. At home the 'haze of females' appeared: he dropped tea trays but he was an excellent pianist. He visited relations. He was tutor for a while in Germany to the children of the hilariously devouring authoress of *Elizabeth and her German Garden*; and astonished a German tutor with his belief that telephone wires were hollow. And then—as was *de rigueur* in his circle—he went off with his mother on momentous cultural tours to Italy and Greece where he, like the ladies of these expeditions, was frugal with his tips and sharply cut them down if any porter or servant complained. (He lived frugally all his life but was wildly generous to his friends and to causes.) On these sentimental journeys in which the Edwardian tourists colonized the pensions and small hotels with their snobberies, moralizings, and their cultural bitching, he became expert in malice.

He, of course, had read up on everything, knew his painting and sculpture, his temples and palaces, and he was a vivid diarist. Pages of dialogue went into the notebooks from which *A Room with a View* and *Where Angels Fear to Tread* were written. But Italy played its ancient trick on him. At Cambridge he had easily shed the Christian religion. Italy confirmed the pagan. His imagination came to life. He experienced almost mystical visions or at any rate sensations of the presence of some primordial and universal beckonings and fatality. The stories of *The Celestial Omnibus* are slight but they relate the devastating effect of metamorphosis upon people dulled or mutilated by respectability. The characters of *Where Angels Fear to Tread* are forced to face pagan passion which is without mercy, and situations in which dull human nature is stripped of pretences and is or is not liberated by acts that shock the foundations of their merely sociable morality. Good and evil are interlaced.

Forster succeeded at once as a novelist. His originality as an observer of character and his daring as a moralist were recognized by the best judges. *Howards End* was a triumph. Here we meet Forster's fear of success, the fear of future sterility. Acclaim put him at a loss for a new subject. There was, he knew, a secret forbidden subject for the truth-teller: his scarcely achieved homosexual desires. All he could do was to console himself by writing erotic stories which he eventually tore up. He was determined to speak out, a good deal because D. H. Lawrence attacked him when they met. He made the disastrous decision to write *Maurice*—disastrous as a step forward in a novelist's life because the book would be unpublishable under British law at that time and would hang like a dead albatross round his neck; even more disastrous because his own experience was distinctly more wishfully sentimental than real. Yet he had to meet the self-accusation that he had been 'tea-tabling' about heterosexual love and marriage while being both a misogynist and an outsider. Lytton Strachey was among those who read the privately circulated manuscript and he saw much to admire. But he wrote:

> I should be inclined to diagnose Maurice's state as simply lust and sentiment—a very wobbly affair; I should have prophesied a rupture after 6 months—chiefly as a result of lack of common interests and owing to class differences ... and so your Sherwood Forest ending appears to me slightly mythical. ... I think he [Maurice] had still a great deal to learn, and that the très-très-noble Alec could never teach it to him. What was wanted was a brief honeymoon with that charming young Frenchman who would have shown Mr Eel that it was possible to take the divagations of a prick too seriously.

We know what followed: he turned to excellent literary criticism and politics. His liberal circles at Cambridge and in Fabian Bloomsbury were hostile to British imperialism in Egypt and India; he wrote for *The Independent Review* and *The New Statesman*; and at the core of his thought was his belief in the primacy of personal relationships: imperialism created the 'bad heart', the crude duty of shutting out intimacy with the ruled. He could afford to travel and, egged on by Masood, a genially fantastic, wilful, and mocking undergraduate who was the ward of the foremost Mohammedan in India in 1912, to soak himself in Indian sights and life.

In Mr Furbank's prolonged accounts of Forster's Indian experience, Forster's engaging letters to his mother enliven a narrative that might otherwise be mere record. One notes that his physical sexual liberation was not to occur until 1916 during the First World War, when he struck out again and worked for the Red Cross in Egypt. Alexandria was the scene of his bizarre, touching, astonishing affair with Mohammed, a miserably poor tram conductor. Strachey would no doubt have called it a 'divagation', but it was well documented by Forster's own notes and in them appears as the happy conflict of the two mocking yet feeling dignities—the dignities of the rich and the abysmally poor. (Rarely in biography do we hear what people really say to each other, but here Furbank can tell us.) Forster felt sexually released; and he had broken through the barriers of class and race. The story of his generous care for Mohammed and of his wife is strange and very moving. After the war was over and Forster had to leave, Mohammed died of illness brought on by the hopeless struggles of the Egyptian poor. Forster had to conceal his breakdown at the news of the death from his mother. One notices his own stern break with his own tears: 'a thing is what it is, and not another thing.'

Being away from his mother for three years and released from 'sexual apprenticeship', Forster returned to find himself under his mother's power once more. They agreed eventually that he might spend two nights away in London every week, but on each free day he sent her a chatty postcard! His dependence on her irked him less as he grew older and his fame as a writer was settled, but we notice the irony. With her, rather than with any man, he was making 'the longest journey' which had made the idea of marriage to a woman horrifying. When she died in 1945 at the age of ninety and he was sixty-six, he wrote to J. R. Ackerley, whose portrait is incidentally very good in this book:

> I wonder whether women are important to one's comfort and stability. I am inclined to think they may be. Although my mother has been intermittently tiresome for the last thirty years, has cramped and warped my genius, hindered my career and buggered up my house, and boycotted my beloved, I have to admit that she provides a sort of rich subsoil where I have been able to rest and grow. That, rather than sex or wifiness, seems to be women's special gift to men.

Still, if he dared not speak out to his mother, he did have one female confidante, the wife of a professor, who was eagerly sympathetic with his homosexual life, a harbinger of contemporary clear-headedness.

Piquant asides relieve the long chronicle. On the serious matter of Forster's second visit to India at the moment of political crisis in 1922 and the writing of *Passage to India* Mr Furbank is very discerning. He gives full attention to the situation in India and to the often angry protests made by distinguished Anglo-Indians, who fell upon Forster's mistakes. He admitted his errors. He agreed that he had only been in India eighteen months in all, but always argued that a novel cannot be judged by its 'fairness'. He wrote to Lowes Dickinson:

> Isn't 'fair-mindedness' dreary! A rare achievement, and a valuable one, you will tell me, but how sterile in one's own soul. I fall in love with Orientals, with Anglo-Indians—no: that is roughly my internal condition, and all the time I had to repress the consequences, or fail to hold the scales. Where is truth? It makes me so sad that I could not give the beloved a better show. One's deepest emotions count for so little as soon

as one tries to describe external life honestly, or even readably. Scarcely anyone has seen that I hoped Aziz would be charming. . . .

An interesting point made by Furbank is that the influence of T. E. Lawrence is marked in the final chapters of the book. Forster admired Lawrence and feared a gang of right-wing people might get hold of him in time.

The diverting and richest aspect of the second visit is the account, drawn from Forster's letters, of his time as the secretary of the delightful, comic, and utterly incompetent Maharajah of Dewas, whose palace and kingdom were falling to pieces. The Maharajah hated catamites though his court was alive with their intrigues, jokes, and whisperings. In a panic Forster got up the courage to confess his tastes to the Maharajah and expected to be sacked. The Maharajah was surprised and felt sorry for him, and rather than encourage him to console himself with masturbation—a great evil because it was lonely—ingeniously arranged for him to have an affair with a court barber. Barbers could come and go without scandal. The comedy is picaresque and instructive.

Further comedies were to occur in Cockney London later on in Forster's life, in a strange local community in which the police had jolly private relations with a lot of minor crooks and others living cheerfully by their wits. This time the *British* class barrier was broken. It is not surprising that Forster regretted he had written *Maurice* before he really knew his subject. The comedy here was harmless. The pity is that it came too late for the novelist. He had become a natural teacher: it was noticed that one or two hefty and wild characters put on solemn cultural airs after their minds had been awakened by his puzzling company.

Forster's own judgement was that the affections were dominant in working men: they were easy about sex, but were not interested in the passion of love. This, one must say, is very sweeping. Yet in this time Forster did have his closest and lasting emotional friendship with Bob Buckingham, then a solid policeman, and his young wife. Just before Forster died Bob apparently denied that the friendship was homosexual and the matter is a mystery, for his wife assumed it was. A strange reversal of the affections occurred in this relationship which has a bearing on Forster's outstanding characteristic—he was generous with money and considerate to a fault: his feeling for the delicacies of personal relationships was tender and endless— and it was the wife who understood him and cared for him when the husband seemed to be bored and cool. The only thing that irritated her was that Forster was untidy and had been used to being waited on by servants.

Why, after *Passage to India*, did Forster write no more novels? He wrote plays that have been lost and, of course, his important *Aspects of the Novel* and the famous *Two Cheers for Democracy*. He played a leading part in campaigns for civil liberties and for intellectual freedom in the Thirties and after. Furbank thinks that although he was a rationalist, Forster was superstitious about the dangers of success. Having been 'royally favoured' as a child he had magical feelings about his own life and would naturally 'have irrational fears at the realization of very deep wishes'. More practically, Forster himself saw that, being homosexual, he had grown bored with writing about love and marriage and the relations of men and women. He must also have felt that in *Maurice* he had written about a homosexual love affair as a substitute for having one. It is probable, Mr Furbank thinks, that he had, though not in the vulgar sense, 'only one novel in him'—'I mean that he received his whole inspiration—a vision, a kind of plot, a message—all at once, in early manhood.'

Still more important, the social types which 'ruled his imagination' were those of his Edwardian youth—which had been made almost brutally out of date by the two wars which destroyed them. Changes move fast today for the novelist.

The common idiom lasts scarcely more than a decade. Also, ruthless as Forster was as a moralist, he had no great powers of invention. Perhaps also one must grant that although his private means did not make him idle, they encouraged his conscience to seek too many targets. Yet his strength as a teacher lay in the refusal to be 'great'. He had the almost magical, gnomic power of making himself inconspicuous while facing with pluck—another favourite word of his—the desperate state of our world.

GRAHAM GREENE

Disloyalties

ENGLISH NOVELISTS ARE not notable for their sense of evil. James Hogg of *The Confessions of a Justified Sinner* has it, and so, in a romantic way, has Stevenson, but both are Scots. Conrad, the Pole, has it; so has Henry James, the American. Among ourselves it is hard to find. There are signs in *Clarissa*; in Dickens evil appears hysterically in the forms of staged melodrama. Only Emily Brontë fully exposes her imagination to the dark spirit and with a pagan or pantheistic exhilaration and pride which profoundly shocked her contemporaries. For Hardy evil is an aloof and alien polity. It can hardly be called more than mischance. The rest of the English novelists settle for a world which must be judged in terms of right and wrong.

Against this Protestant tradition the novels of Graham Greene are a rebellion or, rather, a series of guerrilla ambushes from a Roman Catholic point of view. He was once said to be a Jansenist and was certainly at variance with the accommodating Catholic tradition on the Continent. His religion—as we see it in his early novels—has the egocentricity, the scruple, the puritanism and aggression present in English nonconformity, though it finds more savour in failure than success. God is his misadventure and, for this reason, maybe he is a religious man, i.e. he does not expect to get anything but conflict and pain out of his religion. I must say this is a vast relief after the optimism of the success cults. To the spectator, it seems that Greene wishes to have an adulterer's, a gambler's or a spy's relation with his God and Church, finding more merit in despair than in the laborious conniving at the goodness the ordinary hypocrite goes in for. On the other hand, a man like Scobie, in *The Heart of the Matter*, can hardly rank with the great sinners; he lacks the pride. His muddles and illegalities rate official damnation but, as the priest suggests, there is still God's mercy. His portrait has some of that sentimentality which has come over the Channel from François Mauriac. I doubt if it is fair to Roman Catholic moralists to say that they believe the worst thing is to break the rules.

The light and serious novels of Graham Greene make their impression because of his phenomenal skill, his invention, and the edge and precision of his mind. He etches the conventional with the acid of the observable. His thrillers are not simply escapes from ordinary life, but are painful journeys into it: the agent, hunter or hunted, unveils. In *The Confidential Agent* the true subjects are pain and betrayal. He seeks the exact:

> She lay there stiff, clean and unnatural; people talked as if death were like sleep; it was like nothing but itself. He was reminded of a bird discovered at the bottom of a cage on its back, with the claws rigid as grape stalks: nothing could look more dead. He had seen people dead after an air raid; but they fell in curious humped positions—a lot of embryos in the womb. This was different—a unique position reserved for one occasion. Nobody in pain or asleep lay like this.

In one book at least, *The Power and the Glory*, he transcends his perverse and morbid tendencies and presents a whole and memorable human being; this wholeness is exceptional, for Greene is generally an impressionist, or rather a cutter of mosaics. We expect from incisive talents some kind of diagnosis, some instinctive knowledge of the human situation which we have not attended to; this Greene has had. His subjects are the contemporary loneliness, ugliness and transience. We disapprove of the ugliness of our civilization without recognizing that, for some reason, we *needed* to make it ugly. Greene makes great play with this in his novels; behind the ugliness is loneliness and betrayal. Very nearly all his characters are marked by the loneliness in our civilization, and on the simplest level—Scobie's, for example—they are merely self-pitying. They fail to communicate. Scobie hates talking to his wife because of fear that she will make yet another scene; he knows that talking to his mistress will lead fatally to the re-enacting of the same stale dramas of jealousy. These people wish to be alone; yet when they are alone, the sad dialogues of nostalgia, conscience and betrayal begin in the mind; and presently each character breaks in two: the pursuer and pursued, the watcher and the watched, the hunter and the hunted. The relationship with God, if they are Catholics, is the same. One moment it is God who will have no mercy; next it is Scobie who is torturing God. In *The End of the Affair* the narrator accuses himself of inability to do anything but hate; and Fowler in *The Quiet American* admits that he translates his personal hatred of Pyle and Pyle's dangerous political innocence into a fantastic hatred of the American continent. Loneliness, the failure to communicate in love, or rather to sustain communication, is the cause, and behind that is the first cause, the betrayal we are thought to have experienced in childhood when evil was revealed to us. This is a contemporary subject for, in Greene's rendering of the world, we are now anonymous. We are bleak, observable people in streets, on staircases, in boarding-houses, hotel rooms, cafeterias, Nissen huts, native villages, police stations—free, but disheartened and 'wanted'.

Greene's masterly power of evoking the shabby scene, whether it is Pimlico or Liberia, Mexico or Kent, is a matter of a vision true to its misanthropy and quickness of eye; but it owes something also to his sense of being an accomplice. We are guilty transients leaving our fakes and our litter. There is an odd and frequent suggestion that romantic literature misled us. China, Liberia, Mexico ought not to have looked like this. In the later books, particularly in *The Quiet*

American, the mood has become rather too much the conventional habit of disillusion (assumed for self-protection) of the American school of reporting. In fact only one scene was real reporting, so I have since learned. Only the minor figures observed by the master reporter in the war scenes are individual; the rest have become types. Fowler is mere self-pity; Pyle is a flat profile. There is always a danger in Greene's novels that the stress on banality and anonymity will turn into type-casting and that he will forget that the loneliness of people, on whatever level, is only an aspect of them. In *The Heart of the Matter*, Scobie's scenes with young Mrs Rolt become typical and therefore forced. The sudden leap from pitiable youth to the jealousy of the trained virago on Mrs Rolt's part, makes Greene's point of course, but is too pat. In his honesty he is too eager to see evil doing its stuff.

In *The Power and the Glory*, Greene succeeds above all the rest. In the other tales, by quickness of cinematic cutting, by turning everything he sees to the advantage of action, he makes circles round our doubts. The preposterous argument of *Brighton Rock* is lost in the excitement of the hunt. But in the Mexican novel no doubts arise. There is no overt resentment. There are no innuendos. There are no theological conundrums. It is actually an advantage that Greene hated Mexico and the tropical rot; he had worked the worst off in a vivid book, *The Lawless Roads*. Except for the portrait of the seedy Mr Tench, the dentist, at the beginning, and the account of the Catholic family reading their forbidden literature secretly, there is nothing to distract us from the portraits of the whisky-priest and the lieutenant, his pursuer. In this kind of drama, Mr Greene excels, but here there is meaning, not fear-fantasy; the priest is taken from depth to depth in physical suffering and spiritual humiliation. The climax is reached when he is disowned by his mistress and his child and this long scene is wonderful for the way in which the feeling is manipulated and reversed. The scene in the prison, into which he is thrown by mad misadventure, has to bear the moral burden of the story—that he is at peace with the criminals and outcasts from whom he need not hide his identity, and that he is in danger only from conventional piety. We should not forget that Greene trails his coat in order to provoke mercy and has a subtle and compassionate intelligence of unvoiced pain. As a novelist he is free of the vice of explanation in this book; we see a soul grow and recover its dignity. And the dialogue between the pursuing lieutenant and the priest at the end is a true dialogue; it is not a confrontation of views, but of two lives. The only weakness is in the transition to the Catholic family and the inter-cutting of scenes at the end. I do not know what the intention is. Is it to take us into the starchy world of Catholic piety, into that religious respectability which Greene detests and where, indeed, right and wrong take the place of good and evil? Or is it a return to Greene's boyish love of romantic literature? The child is 'believing' in a boy's heroic adventure in defence of the Faith, as Greene himself might have 'believed' in Rider Haggard. The misanthropy of Greene often reads as if it were a resentment of the deceit of books for boys and a rancour against the loss of the richly populated solitude of childhood.

In *The Comedians* Graham Greene returns to the reporter-novelizing manner of *The Quiet American* and is in a better temper. This book has the usual self-indulgence, the usual zest in the sardonic view. A Greene character has a hard time of it. The couple whom Brown, the present narrator, saw copulating cheerfully in the hotel swimming-pool one night in Haiti could have no notion that he would make a sermon out of them later on, by placing the body of a politician with his wrists cut in the corner of the pool: later still, to ram home the text, the battered head of the same politician will confront yet another woman who kneels down in a garden to be had by a policeman. It is hard luck to be a figure in a parable of sado-masochism.

Another woman—a German whose burden is that her father had been executed for Nazi crimes and who is the mistress of the narrator—fights back against the 'dark brown world you live in'. There is danger, you see, even in Brown's name. Having got out of bed and sworn at her suspender, she gives him a lecture.

> To you nothing exists except in your own thoughts. Not me, not Jones. We're what you choose to make us. You're a Berkeleyan. My God, what a Berkeleyan. . . . My dear, try to believe we exist when you aren't there. We're independent of you. None of us is like what you fancy we are. Perhaps it wouldn't matter much if your thoughts were not so dark, always so dark.

She is right. She has even accused him of being a novelist. And she is right again. In so many of his novels Graham Greene makes an overwhelming and literary intervention so that his people are reduced to things seen flat in the camera's eye and by the cleverest of living photographers. It is true that the author's mind is courageous, charitable and compassionate: no character can complain that he has not been enhanced in the very instant of being flattened or narrowed—and to say that is to say a great deal for Greene as an artist. If he piles it on, he does so with the inner gaiety of a great talent. But one often wishes that he were less of a contriver and would let the characters show for themselves what their meaning is. That passage about Berkeley is unlikely in the mouth of the German refugee wife of a diplomat in Haiti; it annuls her as an independent human being and breaks the novel's illusion. Not only that, one suspects the speech is there as an essayist's insurance against the suspicion that elsewhere, in the 'piled-on' incidents, Greene is parodying himself as a novelist. And perhaps as a conceit or a joke.

The theme of the novel is put by a priest preaching on the

text: 'Let us go up to Jerusalem and die with him'. Indifference is to be condemned more harshly than violence. 'Violence can be the expression of love, indifference never. One is an imperfection of charity, the other the perfection of egoism'. The indifferent are the comedians, i.e. the egoists, in a tragic world. (It is odd to see indifference presented as the antithesis of violence; but I suppose we are back at that barbarous Manichean idea expressed in 'Because ye are neither hot nor cold' etc. etc.) The chief comedian is Brown himself, a lapsed Catholic speculator who has never known his father, was born in the no man's land of Monte Carlo and now runs a tourist hotel in Haiti. He has inherited it from his mother, a decent, now elderly tart found living with her black servant: she dies—need one say—after one last fling of intercourse. The black servant is so upset he hangs himself.

Brown had left Haiti, partly because of his possessive jealousy of his mistress, the diplomat's wife; now he returns to the disgusting police state and to the murdered politician. The horrible condition of this *triste tropique* is sharply evoked. No one so powerfully burns an exotic and seedy scene on the mind. Haiti is an island run by faceless Negro and mulatto crooks in sun-glasses. In Port-au-Prince arrives a farcical pair of American innocents, one-time freedom-riders, all for justice, who wish to persuade the government to open a vegetarian centre. The cranks are slow-motion slapstick, but they have their courage and dignity. They are also—in a business way—shrewd: this, and one or two adroit observations of their affectionate hypochondria, redeem them from pure caricature. They pass harmlessly from the scene—one can see that Brown's hotel had to have at least a couple of residents—to make way for a merry little spiv called Jones, self-styled hero of the Burma war, semi-secret agent, speculator, petty gambler, stoic, self-advertised Don Juan, and an instant friend of Papa Doc, the bloody dictator; selling out on him, however, he joins a Resistance group in the mountains.

Jones is a *comic* comedian—he is committed to making something out of the anarchy that the deeply comic are drawn into. It turns out that he has lied about everything—he is, in fact, wanted internationally for theft—but his lies catch up with him and he is forced to lead the guerrillas in the mountains because his bluff is called. Why do the Resistance people take him on? Because he is so irresistible. He makes people laugh. He has no real notion of what he is doing, beyond perhaps being a bit awestruck by people of principle. Eventually his feet let him down in the rough country. It is a surprising weakness that one has the death of Jones by hearsay; also that of Dr Magiot, the sad, upright Marxist who has managed to survive because communists are useful political counters: they enable Papa Doc to blackmail the Americans.

In this context of secret shootings, beatings-up and dejected plotting, in which the Haitians have either the brutal or the dedicated parts, Brown and his mistress conduct their private sexual comedy, in momentary beddings in the backs of cars, and in a grave-like hollow under the trees. They are nervous of discovery; Brown thinks his mistress's child may be spying on them. It is an affair constantly on edge because of his possessive nagging jealousies—Greene is always on the *qui vive* for the ironies of impotence and desire. And of betrayal. Treachery has always been one of Greene's central preoccupations as a moralist. Brown betrays Jones because he is jealous, by working cynically on his vanity; and the irony is that Jones, the liar, is the better man. His life could be construed, Brown suddenly sees, as a series of delinquent approaches to virtue. Such paradoxes fit in admirably with Greene's gift for creating suspense.

Brown is cool enough in danger, but he is a born destroyer of his own and his mistress's happiness. It is he who is really the absurd figure because all his suspicions turn out to be untrue: he has so little perception of normal feelings. Jones, the shady liar, is capable of inspiring affection. Brown, the

adulterer, is so tied-up that he inspires pity. But Brown *thinks*—
it is noticeable how often the heroes of the reporter's novel are
Hamlets, tortured by the guilt of being outside, of having kept
an escape-route, as they knowingly rock their pink gin in the
glass and misanthropically bitch their Ophelias—and guilt
sharpens even while it perverts observation. He has one
exciting episode—Greene at his best—in which he smuggles
Jones out to his rendezvous. The moment in which the awful
police chief—admirably called Concasseur—is shot and has his
sun-glasses trodden on is very fine. That is the kind of detail
that reconciles us to Greene when we are just about to cry
parody again.

The end of *The Comedians* is, like the beginning, a sardonic
essay. The vegetarian Americans are in San Domingo and, in
their grateful and businesslike way, they get Brown a partner-
ship in a funeral business where the drift of local politics offers
growing prospects. This is a nasty but exact diagnosis; the
speciousness lies in our feeling that the symbolism is being
piled on and that the people are puppets in an animated
disquisition. The effect is literary. We have been reading news
and news leaves us with the sense of waste. But as San
Domingo follows Haiti, as Nigeria distracts us from the
Congo, Greene has obviously chosen an important subject;
and though he is an outsider, there are moments in which he
gets inside. The Voodoo scene in which we watch a sensitive
man being turned by grotesque religious performance into a
partisan catches a note of tropical excess.

> The priest came in from his inner room swinging a censer, but
> the censer which he swung in our faces was a trussed cock—
> the small stupid eyes peered into my eyes and the banner of St
> Lucy swayed after it. When he had completed the circle of the
> *tonelle* the *hougan* put the head of the cock in his mouth and
> crunched it cleanly off; the wings continued to flap while the
> head lay on the dirt-floor like part of a broken toy. Then he
> bent down and squeezed the neck like a tube of tooth-paste

and added the rusty colour of blood to the ash-grey patterns on the floor.

But I think he overcrowds with the apparatus of horror; and especially in the sexual incident, one begins to grin and even to laugh.

Greene is laughing too, but we are at cross purposes; we are laughing at self-parody as we laugh at melodrama and he is laughing at his own pleasure in giving more and more turns to what, in both senses, is the screw. Brown is supposed to have lost his faith and to be adrift because he has found nothing to replace it. Yet in fact he *has* found something: the hotel-keeper has ostensibly written this remarkable book. That is an act of faith; certainly not an act of indifference. Or didn't Brown write the book? Is it all a game? All virtuosi are entitled to indulge their talents. But when Greene wrote *The Power and the Glory* he was not playing a game.

How many of his now huge audience know him in the very different role of the bookish man or as a literary critic and essayist? He has gone through the English mill. His *Collected Essays* contain a selection of these writings done mainly for the London weeklies or as introductions, during the last thirty years; there are also a traveller's portraits of two Popes, Philby, Ho Chi Minh, Castro and others. All display the well-known concerns which have given him originality and verve as a novelist; all—or nearly all—have the final sympathy which a real curiosity about human nature deposits in an observant mind.

In the manner of English periodical criticism where the writer has to get at an essence, show his wit and his hand, and make his decisive effect with alacrity in fewer than 2000 scrupulous words, Greene engages at once: 'A man must be judged by his enemies as well as by his friendships'. Himself he cannot resist the attractions of the enemy. He is before any-thing a novelist-critic, that is to say he writes to discover something for *his* purposes which might not be ours. His reviews are an artist's raids; he has the avid eye of the raider and will often pause before the corpse of his victim to note a quality or to ask what went wrong.

He has a cheerful, almost cannibal appetite for rationalists. For him, rationalists, figures like Samuel Butler and Havelock Ellis, are conceited and emotionally arid; then, among rhetoricians he cannot forgive Kipling; among sentimentalists, Barrie. Of the 'greatly gifted they are the two who have written with most falsity of human relationships'. Unresolved hatreds or infantile secrets have ruined them. Butler has the smugness of the Honest Man: 'Even Christianity would not be considered dispassionately because it is the history of a Father and a Son'. Herbert Read, who had hailed so many fashions in painting and literature, had himself supplied (in his grave books on childhood and his *Life* of Wordsworth) the 'standards of permanence by which these fashions will be condemned'. Whether they add or ruffle, Greene's opinions have an artist's necessity in them. Let the academics weigh up, be exhaustive, or build their superstructures—the artist lives as much by his pride in his own emphasis as by what he ignores; humility is a disgrace.

Greene has a marked loyalty to writers who have influenced him and to those who are out of fashion. He is free of the snobbery that pretends it has had no time for the juvenile or second rate. The books of boyhood—Ballantine, Hope, Mason, Weyman, Rider Haggard and the *Viper of Milan*—were decisive for him: two or three themes, central in Greene's own writing, expand from them. Exotic, thrilling adventure, the lost childhood and its betrayal, the warnings against success, the lure of perfect evil. In the *Viper of Milan* he thinks he saw

> Perfect evil walking the world, where perfect good can never walk again, and only the pendulum ensures that after all in the end justice is done.

Life is not black and white; it is black and grey. After *The Power and the Glory, The Comedians.*

This theme was fulfilled when he confronted Henry James, Conrad—and equally important to him I would guess later on —Ford Madox Ford. Apart from anything else they are master craftsmen and, in all these reviews, we see Greene's concern with how things are done. He himself is, above all, skilled and eagerly interested in difficulty. But the importance of Henry James is the concern with supernatural evil, the nervous venture to the edge of religion; in the detection of the 'black and merciless things that lie behind great possessions'; in corruption and betrayal. This is far from being the whole of James, but the subject draws out the four most studied essays in the collection. In the Thirties, Greene was allured by the James who could conceive the damned soul and who might just have become a Catholic if his father had not exhausted the subject of an organized church. But, by the Fifties, looking at *Guy Domville*, he writes:

> To us today the story of Guy Domville seems . . . one more example of the not always fortunate fascination exercised on James by the Christian faith and by Catholicism.

Is there such a thing as agnostic prose? May not a rationalist be fully conscious of mental degradation or good and evil? Wasn't James?

The search for the seat of unease in his subject is Greene's point in a great many of these essays. There are eighty of them. Conrad Aiken, pushing the study of madness to its limits in *King Coffin* 'is the most satisfying of living novelists'; in Walter de la Mare's stories—now absurdly underrated or forgotten— we meet the terrified eyes of a fellow passenger 'watching the sediment of an unspeakable obsession'; of Rolfe—whose *Hadrian the Seventh* is a work of genius—he writes: 'if he could not have Heaven he would have Hell and the last footprints seem to point to the Inferno'. The unease was not always gratefully acknowledged. One would have thought his delightful and affectionate essay on Beatrix Potter's tales written in 1933 would have pleased the authoress; we imagine she would have given a thunderstruck grin when Greene's King Charles's head popped up at the climax among the bunnies and the puddle-ducks:

> Looking back over the thirty years of Miss Potter's literary career, we see that the creation of Jemima Puddle-Duck marked the beginning of a new period. At some time between 1907 and 1909 Miss Potter must have passed through an emotional ordeal which changed the character of her genius. It would be impertinent to enquire into the nature of the ordeal. Her case is curiously similar to that of Henry James. Something happened which shook their faith in appearance. From *The Portrait of a Lady* onwards, innocence deceived, the treachery of friends, became the theme of James's greatest stories. Mme Merle, Kate Croy, Mme de Vionnet, Charlotte Stant these tortuous, treacherous women, are paralleled through the dark period of Miss Potter's art. 'A man can smile and be a villain', that, a little altered, was her recurrent message . . . with the publication of *Mr Tod* in 1912 Miss Potter's pessimism reached its climax.

An acid letter from Miss Potter—who had become a tough sheep-farmer in Westmorland—was the reward for this grand analysis. She was, she said, suffering from no emotional disturbance when she wrote *Mr Tod*: only the after effects of flu. She said she deprecated 'the Freudian school' of criticism. Perhaps the comparison with another artist annoyed the old lady. She was certainly cross when *Little Pig Robinson* was described by Mr Greene as being her *Tempest*: he called it her last tale when it was the first written, if not the first published. But as we know now, from Margaret Lane's *Life* and the published *Journals*, there had been two extreme crises in her life and an extraordinary change of personality. Graham Greene had been an expert detective.

The collection covers a reviewer's wide field. Anthony à Wood, some Oxford eccentrics, Evelyn, Charles Churchill, Darley, Fielding, Sterne are among his subjects and done with care and point. The novelist is botanizing in human character; the traveller is absorbed by Parkman, Livingstone, Mungo Park; there is a fierce attack on J. B. Trend's book on Mexico, for though Trend was a conventional and timid Cambridge professor he was a violent anti-Catholic. (But he did write a very valuable if innocent book on Spain in the Twenties.) Greene's final essay on a sentimental return to Lagos, the Scobie country, in 1968, has the nostalgia for a lost innocence which encases much of his work, nostalgia for a lost innocence never quite as innocent as it looked. In Lagos, last year (in church, one gathers),

the girl in front of me wore one of the surrealist Manchester cotton dresses which are rarely seen since the Japanese trade moved in. The word 'soupsweet' was printed over her shoulder, but I had to wait until she stood up before I could confirm another phrase: 'Fenella lak' good poke'. Father Mackie would have been amused, I thought, and what better description could there be of this poor lazy lovely coloured country than 'soupsweet'.

In all his moods, angry, serious or laughing, Greene has the patient precise eye of the connoisseur of 'brief lives'.

EVELYN WAUGH

Club and Country

MANY GOOD WRITERS live on their nerves and can turn to anything. Clever, they have only one self. This is not the case with Evelyn Waugh; he has many selves, deeply embedded, on which to draw. He might have settled down with Lady Metroland and tippled away at a mixture of the *Bab Ballads*, the cautionary tale and Firbank; but his real line was the prose, not the poetry, of outrage. The wild, feathered feminine scream of that last master was not for him. His temperament was sober. He moved to the hard-headed traditions of English satirical comedy; one glance at the English upper classes, imposing their private fantasies on whatever is going on, treating everything from war downwards as if it were all happening in one of their country houses, has been enough to provide comedians with material for a lifetime. Mr Waugh went on next to be inconvenienced by his Sir Galahad and St George complexes; but after *Brideshead Revisited* and a brief return to the outrageous in *The Loved One*, the gentleman moralist appeared, a clubbish writer assiduously polishing his malign sentences, daily persisting with the stings of mortifying circumlocution. His early books spring from the liberating notion that human beings are mad; the war trilogy, a work of maturity, draws on the meatier notion that the horrible thing about human beings is that they are sane.

For better or worse, there is a masculine vein in English comedy, a vein which is sociable and not intellectual, sensible rather than sensitive. It shows us willingly paying the price of misanthropy for the pleasure of making a go of life in clubs— day and night—parsonages, public schools, villas, furnished apartments and other privacies of the national masochism. It required a nerve on Mr Waugh's part to treat the war as something which could or could not be known socially in these terms. It also required the accomplishment of a lifetime to bring off those three volumes. It is true that they have the formal melancholy of a memoir, and that Sir Galahad strikes a few unattractive poses; but the comic invention is strong: and there is an advance towards a compassionate study of human nature. Crouchback's bad wife would once have been seen as a vile body; she is now discerned as a displaced person.

The melancholy note persists in the first volume of Mr Waugh's autobiography, *A Little Learning*. In his dire way he has done what he can to pass himself off as a fossil. Like his father—as he appears in this volume—the son is a considerable impersonator. His prose is set to the felicities of misleading. This book is of great importance to students of his novels— though he does not yet discuss them—for it shows how long-established his preoccupations as a man and writer have been. An outstanding quality of his work has been its care for cadence in English prose and his regard for craftsmanship as a moral duty; he comes of a line of clergy and doctors, some of whom were minor writers; his background is literary and un-assumingly sedate. The youthful taste for working at medieval script is another sign of the craftsman to come and a sign too of that feeling for Romance which has been the less successfully manifested aspect of his work. (His father was also romantic; he would refer to the 'stout timbers' of the villa he built for himself as if it were some galleon anchored in the North End Road and never forgave the local authorities for incorporating his then rustic part of Hampstead into the ugly and socially ambiguous brashness of new Golders Green.)

As for religion, Mr Waugh was always interested in theology and never at all bored by church. There is nothing to suggest that his later conversion to Catholicism was Romantic;

everything to suggest that theological ingenuity was an important appeal. A relative in the Bengal Lancers brought in the St George touch and the nostalgia for swords and regalias. The designs of the nursery wallpaper were medieval: it was a taste of the period. The boy's upbringing was quiet, instructed, entirely happy. No Oedipal struggles appear. There was nothing to provoke the later sense of outrage, nothing—apparently—to titillate the psychiatrist except the mildness of it all. Even at the end of the volume, when he plans to drown himself after coming down from Oxford, full of debts and depressed about lost fun, Mr Waugh takes the view that this was a normal adolescent gesture, abandoned at once when he swam into some jellyfish.

What provoked the taste for outrage? Mr Waugh is a thoughtful rather than an intimate autobiographer, in this volume. He keeps the lid on. His aim appears to be the desire to conform, no doubt ironically, to a carefully prepared conventional pattern and to repose, almost masochistically, upon a belief in the Unremarkable. Clearly this, in so dashing an imagination, suggests a conflict. His marvellous feel for the disreputable comes from a man with a family addiction to the neutral yet aspiring. But one thing *did* go wrong. There was no woodshed. But home was so happy that to leave it for school made him 'nastier' (on the general principle that all schoolboys are 'nasty'?). And then there was the despoiling of England.

As one who belongs to his generation, though coming from a very different background, I understand something of what Mr Waugh means when he writes of the shock caused by the ruin of rural England. It would seem all the worse to a literary suburban:

This is part of the grim cyclorama of spoliation which surrounded all English experience in this century and my understanding of the immediate past (which presumably is the motive for reading a book such as this) must be incomplete unless this huge deprivation of the quiet pleasure of the eye is accepted as a dominant condition, sometimes making for impotent resentment, sometimes for mere sentimental apathy, sometimes poisoning love of country and of neighbours. To have been born into a world of beauty, to die amid ugliness, is the common fate of all us exiles.

The evil, then, was the sense of exile. Most, indeed I would say all writers, have this sense anyway. It was exacerbated for him, as for many schoolboys, by the frustration of 'being out of the war'. It was his brother Alec Waugh, not Evelyn, who would be the hero. One was reduced to dreamy, hungry, insubordinate futility. In some respects Mr Waugh's exile is snobbish. Mr Waugh, senior, was an industrious and kindly reviewer of the old school who hated the new thing in the best jocose tradition of elderly criticism; Mr Waugh, junior, turns rancorous: 'There are the State-trained professional critics with their harsh jargon and narrow tastes.' Mr Waugh senior has his jargon too. Of D. H. Lawrence's art he wrote: 'his fancy is half asleep upon a foetid hot-bed of moods.' But, as his son truly says, as a critic the elder Waugh was no snob. His limitation was the 'common enough inability to recognise the qualities he loved unless they were presented in familiar forms'. Mr Waugh's own 'State-trained' reveals a similar inability.

Prep school, public school, university: these now tedious influences standardize English autobiography, giving the educated Englishman the sad if fascinating appearance of a stuffed bird of sly and beady eye in some odd seaside museum. The fixation on school has become a class trait. It manifests itself as a mixture of incurious piety and parlour game. (Some of Mr Waugh's contemporaries are now writing or have written their autobiographies and are watching each other like chess-players. What was Rugby doing when Sherborne saw Waugh go to Lancing and did Eton care?)

Cautious, lonely, observant at first at Oxford, Mr Waugh

eventually kicked out, did the right thing by drinking a lot and coming down deep in debt, and was ready for a far more interesting life than appears in this opening volume. One must hope that his feeling for impersonality will not become so subtle as to make the irony too sober. The best things in the present volume are those that recover the detail of a period. One recognizes this room:

> The dining-room was dark and full of oil-paintings. The drawing-room was much cluttered with small tables, draperies, screens and ornaments on carved brackets. It contained two cabinets full of 'curiosities'—fans, snuff-boxes, carved nuts, old coins and medals; some of them unremarkable, such as, carefully wadded, encased and labelled, the charred tip of a walking stick with which some relation had climbed Mount Vesuvius and a lock [unauthenticated] of Wordsworth's hair.

There was even a phial containing a specimen of 'White Blood' from a patient dying of anaemia. Tourists' trophies had not yet become standardized.

Mr Waugh is a master also of the compressed portrait. There are three maiden aunts—an extinct genus now, as Mr Waugh points out:

> My Aunt Connie sat on the bench when women became eligible as magistrates and was much distressed by the iniquities there revealed to her. All three had the prudishness proper to maiden aunts, though Aunt Elsie in old age developed a tolerance of very slightly indelicate fiction.

The portrait is good, the prose embroidered here with the facetious parlance—is that the word?—of clubs. This is the trouble with club Mandarin—it becomes flunkeyish. Better write like Wooster than like Jeeves. The crisp manner used in describing W. W. Jacobs is preferable:

In person he was wan, skinny, sharp-faced, with watery eyes. Like many humorists he gave scant evidence of humour in private intercourse. In losing the accents of Wapping he lost most of his voice and spoke through the side of his thin lips in furtive, almost criminal tones, disconcerting in a man of transcendent, indeed of tedious respectability. He was a secular puritan, one of those who 'have not got the Faith and will not have the fun'. . . .

Except for the last sentence, the portrait is exact. The little man was skipping up and down, as merry as popcorn, when I once caught sight of him at a suburban 'hop'. It must be remembered that all humorists suffer from overwork.

The gentle portrait of the author's father is the longest in the book. It is interesting chiefly as an example of a quality that is generally overlooked by admirers of the son's comic originality. The wit, the hilarious transitions, the pace and savagery of his comedies, deceives us into seeing Mr Waugh as a writer who jumps with inspired carelessness from one fantasy to the next. The dialogue alone, his early forte, should undeceive us. Its quality is accuracy; in fact a grave exactitude has been the ground of his comic genius as it is of his serious writing in travel and biography. He can be accurate to the point of testiness. Indeed he is only bad when he is not accurate, that's to say when St George, panache etc. come in and make him slur.

Mr Waugh's eye for the fact enables him to catch the changing impressions so important to the faithful memorialist. Until he was sixteen he had supposed that his father was simple and prosaic; then a friend came down and said: 'Charming, entirely charming and acting all the time'. He was. Between bouts of coughing he would cheerfully call upon Death for release; declare in the middle of signing a cheque he was being driven to a pauper's grave. He talked aloud to imaginary people continuously. He assumed, without knowing it, Dickensian roles. Before the 'ingratitude' of his sons he became Lear. His sighs could be heard across a theatre. He had talent as an amateur actor and, on the evidence of his son's prose—on the confessions of Pinfold and the anecdotes that trickle down from the West Country about his histrionic mischief—one would guess that Evelyn Waugh's sobriety is a genuine impersonation. It is unsafe to trust the elegiac tone of this volume; he may also be trying out his own funeral in advance, to see what a literary demise could look like. Autobiography is a way of dressing up the past.

So far we have been reading about the unknown Evelyn Waugh. In the last chapter the frosts of youth vanish; the young sparkler appears. We see contemporaries who were later to become famous or notorious, among them Gerald Gardiner, Harold Acton, Robert Byron and Brian Howard. Of the last two we have striking, not to say pungent, preliminary sketches. Brian Howard, particularly, was one of those dangerous, destructive and seminal nuisances, a plaguing character of wasted talent who begins to barge about in the corridors of Mr Waugh's early fancy. Grimes turns up in Wales, an effusively homosexual schoolmaster. We have reached the verge of *Decline and Fall*, when Mr Waugh began to rise and shine.

*   *   *

With *Unconditional Surrender* Evelyn Waugh brought his wartime trilogy and Guy Crouchback's love affair with military servitude to a civil end. The infatuation had begun in *Men at Arms*. It was romantic, strenuous and hilarious, set in the glorious days of the Molotov–Ribbentrop treaty when Crouchback, a Catholic gentleman, no longer very young, was being taught to polish his sword and train for a St George-and-Dragon battle with the fundamental enemy: 'the Modern Age', i.e. everything between the days the family property went in the reign of Elizabeth I and the Nazi–Communist pact. He joined the Halberdiers, hung about Bellamy's Club. The comedies of military discipline and chicanery absorbed him; the tedium was relieved by minor campaigns, the war about Apthorpe's portable thunder box, his liability to bouts of 'Bechuana tummy'. Apthorpe was one of Waugh's richest comic creations.

The next phase—*Officers and Gentlemen*—was ambiguous. The Communists were on our side now and that rather muddled St George's objective. Also, a number of officers who were not gentlemen turned up—the shady and resourceful ex-hairdresser, Trimmer, for example. Bellamy's still stood but Turtle's, further down St James's, caught fire in the Blitz and the whisky poured down the street. Air Marshal Beech, not quite our class, was found over-staying an air raid under a billiard table. There were exercises on a Scottish island where the far-seeing Laird, choked by peat smoke in his Castle, was intriguing for supplies of gelignite for a private purpose. He had a daughter who was pro-Hitler and got Crouchback into prolonged trouble. Trimmer, in these rough days, was looking for a woman and picked up Guy Crouchback's ex-wife, a nymphomaniac, and, later on—being a ranker-officer—behaved with absurd cowardice on a Commando raid. For this he naturally became a national hero—the Press having been told to find one in order to impress our doubting Allies, the Americans. Later, in Crete, Crouchback experienced disaster. His *liaison dangereuse* with the military dragged on between farce, boredom, status quarrels, and ended in a few days of nightmare. He escaped from Crete in an open boat.

At the beginning of *Unconditional Surrender*, Crouchback's apathy is complete; but his capacity for pain has been noted by the gods. He persuades himself that it is his duty to remarry his ex-wife because she is going to have a child by the gaudy Trimmer who, punch-drunk with international publicity, has vanished. After a period of parachute training under another ranker, Ludovic, who—again, no gentleman—has murdered his C.O. in the flight from Crete, Crouchback is nagged by an ex-schoolmaster in Yugoslavia. On top of that there is the double-dealing of partisan warfare. He is obliged to watch helplessly the persecution of a party of homeless Jews and to see his discreet attempt to better the lot of two of them turn into the lunatic evidence that will send them to the People's Court and the firing squad. Crouchback's apathy breaks when he realizes that a sense of the futility of life is not enough, for life has culminated in the monstrous. It is perhaps the final, mortifying irony of the book that Crouchback survives and prospers. He even has the pleasure of seeing Box-Bender, his extremely unlikeable Protestant brother-in-law, having trouble with his son. The boy talks of becoming a monk.

Evelyn Waugh has a genius for very specialized social effrontery and its delight in outrage. It required a nerve to treat the war as a sordid social jamboree of smart and semi-smart sets, who are mainly engaged in self-inflation and in climbing up the ladder, to present it as a collection of bank-rupt sideshows. But Mr Waugh has more nerve than any of his English contemporaries, and large portions of the last war were exactly as he describes them.

The war is not, of course, presented as anything more than heightened (or deflated) personal experience; the trilogy is a memoir rather than a novel. Other books about the war have gone straight for the conventional—the battle. He, too, can negligently turn out a battle, but his interest is, fundamentally, the moralist's. His eye is trained on the flat detail of human folly, vanity and hypocrisy; and although he can be rightly called a wounded Romantic, he is a most patient and accurate observer. His glances at London life during the period are laconic and just. The last war saw the birth of the organization man and Mr Waugh was in, all eyes and ears, at the dreadful *accouchement*.

There are, we know, two Evelyn Waughs: the satirical

blessing who wrote *The Loved One* and the appeasing, even tender comic moralist, the accomplished, testy, courteous, epigrammatic man of letters who wrote *A Handful of Dust.* (Crouchback characteristically takes Anstey's *Vice Versa* to read on his campaigns.) The trilogy is in his humane and perfectly finished manner. His scorn is modulated, his sentences are distillations. Most comic writers like to think they could play it straight if only their public would let them. Waugh is able to be grave without difficulty for he has always been comic for serious reasons. He has his own, almost romantic sense of propriety. His snobbery, when he is in this mood, is an amusing and acceptable mixture of High Romance, Puritan decorum and tartness, and has a professional sense of the rules of the English class game. To object to his snobbery is as futile as objecting to cricket, for every summer the damn game comes round again whether you like it or not.

Only one kind of snobbery is affronting in Mr Waugh: the violent. It is ugly, theatrical and falsely generalized. Even if we accept that ranker-officers are envious, calculating, unsure showmen and on the make, must we add cowardice, lack of nerve and—as in the case of the minutely observed Ludovic—crime? Is the envy of the lower classes any more likely to lead to dishonesty and cowardice than the conceit of the uppers? It is here that Mr Waugh's High Romance becomes vulgar sentimentality. In this book he throws Ludovic away as a recognizable human being and an original type rarely attempted: the solemn, climbing, half-sinister, half-hurt queer with shattering gifts as a bad writer. I do not deny that Mr Waugh uses him with malign masochistic skill when he shows him writing a novel that falsifies a good deal of Crouchback's experience, for Ludovic has watched Crouchback like a cat.

Amid the antics of brigadiers, generals, politicians, socialites, partisans, wives and mistresses, the dry and stoical Crouchback is a frosty figure. His apathy makes him a perfect focus. He is given a nullity that, on the one hand, may represent the gentlemanly ideal: the whole of life will be vulgar to him. On the other hand, he is subtly endowed with the reticence and decency that suggest a life profoundly satisfied by the pains that have been inflicted on it, and by the one or two affections that remain.

Virginia, the faithless wife and good-time girl, is beautifully understood. The comedy of her conversation, full of four letter words, with the almost virginal Uncle Peregrine is exquisite. He had never heard a lady use such language; it astounds rather than displeases; it also misleads, for he has the flattering illusion that she is making a pass at him and is piqued when he finds she is not. What she is after is re-marriage to her ex-husband who has come into money, for she is at the end of her tether. It is the measure of Mr Waugh's sympathy that he lets out no savage laugh at the cynical proposition and yet is not sentimental about it. The war has, at any rate, taught Crouchback to recognize a 'displaced person' when he sees one. He does not love her. She does not love Trimmer's child when it is born: she calls it 'that baby'. Crouchback does not weep when she is killed in an air raid, which lets him off some of the awkward consequences of playing so straight a bat in the sex Test. And when, at the end of one novel, his awful brother-in-law complains that things have turned very conveniently for Guy, we muse happily on the richness of Mr Waugh's point. His comedy has always been hard, perverse and shocking; but that in no way prevents it from reproducing the human heart with delicacy, or at any rate, that portion of the heart that, however shallow, can still feel wrong and pain.

Only two episodes in this final volume strike me as being tame: the strange, dull set-piece when Ludovic files past the Sword of Stalingrad in Westminster Abbey. As symbolism, irony, fragment of war chronicle, whatever it is, this scene is in the way. Later on, Ludovic goes to a party given by the editor of a literary monthly whose grubby camel-hair coat and sharp

Sultanic orders to the girls will bring back sentimental memories to knowing readers; but again, this is a tame jest. The vanities of the military and social servitudes are Mr Waugh's subject; it is good, of course, of Mr Waugh to call and all that on his Bohemian friends, but somehow the visit falls flat. No literary figure can compete with an Apthorpe, a Trimmer, an Uncle Peregrine or any of the huge list of exquisitely touched-in characters who fought the war with chits, passes and top secret reports, in Mr Waugh's terse *Who's Who* of the National Peril.

St George Crouchback ends by reassessing his views on the dragon. Mme Kanyi, a Hungarian Jewess, says to him:

'Is there any place that is free from evil? It is too simple to say that the Nazis wanted war. These Communists wanted it too. It was the only way in which they could come to power. Many of my people wanted it, to be revenged on the Germans, to hasten to the creation of the national state. It seems to me there was a will to war, a death wish, everywhere. Even good men, thought their private honour would be satisfied by war. They could assert their manhood by killing and being killed. They would accept hardships in recompense for having been selfish and lazy. Danger justified privilege. I knew Italians—not very many perhaps—who felt this. Were there none in England?'

'God forgive me,' said Guy, 'I was one of them.' It was after being told, by an enthusiastic little bureaucrat, of her arrest, that Crouchback was tempted to strike an officer.

ANGUS WILSON

Going Downhill

IT IS 'OUR LIFE', says one of the characters in Angus Wilson's ambitious early novel *Anglo-Saxon Attitudes*, that lies between ourselves and reality. It is a novel about the conscience as it worries two generations of a middle-class family whose ample money comes out of steel and whose brains have gone into the academic world and popular politics. The title comes from Lewis Carroll who noticed—and who with better reason?— that the attitudes of the Anglo-Saxon were peculiar; they are formed by an incalculable mixture of going one's own gait and contorting oneself in the gymnasium of the English moral sense. Morally the English are liable to picturesque outbursts of self-deception: being intelligent, we are very conscious of this and if this is decadent it is also very interesting. When we say (as we have often said during the last thirty years), 'What right have we to judge him or her?', we know quite well that we are going to be led to awful questions, the conundrum of the greater or the lesser evil, the blandishments of the wider view, and so on. The countrymen of Lewis Carroll and George Eliot are born worriers; the relieving thing about them is that they are also an awkward squad, bad at drill, prone to brutal jokes, underhand tricks, romantic sensuality, poker-faced wangling and the smug exploitation of lucky accident. Show me a Puritan and I will (thank God) show you a rogue. At the back of the lives of Mr Angus Wilson's characters there is a dirty Anglo-Saxon trick—scabrous, silly, but rich in moral provocation. What more could we, who live on moral tension, desire?

As far as his novel is concerned, this angry practical joke is a useful device. It is full of symbolism which is a bore, but it has enabled Mr Wilson to begin with some excellent comedy about academic life among historians and archaeologists. As far as the general theme is concerned his joke is no more than a Gibbonian footnote. When the novel opens in the present day, the historians can still be set quarrelling about the discovery of a phallic object which was found in the coffin of the Saxon Bishop Eorpwald when he was dug up in 1912. It has not greatly disturbed the layman to suppose that Christians may have lapsed into paganism: after all, pagans had already lapsed into Christianity. But the Eorpwald discovery had sent one poor scholarly lady out of her mind: she connected it with Baltic trade and, thence, fatally, to the 'wider view'. There is more than a hint that the original discoverer, the eminent Lionel Stokesay, became very odd afterwards and certainly morally senile. He began to talk like Ramsay MacDonald. The probability is that people who take the wider view are covering up.

In the opening chapter of *Anglo-Saxon Attitudes* we are to understand that the Eorpwald row has died down and that it remains open only in the minds of cranks. On the other hand, the central character of the book, Gerald Middleton, a sixty-year-old historian who was Lionel Stokesay's disciple and his son's friend, becomes suspiciously irritable when the subject is reopened. For him, it reawakens what he is least inclined to examine: the errors of his life, the failure to go the full length of his talents, above all the failure of his will. He is a true Anglo-Saxon: he has a romantic sense of failure as well as a romantic sense of success. (I am not sure that Mr Angus Wilson is with us here.) At any rate, Middleton thinks—and so does Mr Wilson—that he has sacrificed reality or truth to 'his life'. For Middleton has the strongest reasons for suspecting that a serious fraud was committed by Stokesay's famous, destructive, sadistic and short-lived son at the time of the discovery. Middleton has kept silence in the interests of the old man's reputation. Moreover, Middleton's great love was for the younger Stokesay's wife. In these terms, Middleton's silence is a symptom of his general moral guilt and weakness, which make him accept a bad marriage instead of a difficult love; which force him to prolong the marriage for the sake of his children whom he nevertheless alienates and who are not going to respect him later; which drives his mistress to drink while he plumps for urbanity, compromise, rational marital arrangements, the limitation of his talents, intellectual indolence and picture-collecting—this last is unbecoming in a scientist and a scholar. (Puritanism will out: enjoyment of the arts by people with private means is morally suspect.) Middleton is saddled with money as well and has really bought his way out of his troubles—as many do who have *no* money—and now, at sixty, isolated by his habit of refusing life, he is left to look back upon the ruins of his life and to see his children infected by his mistakes. In the end, he gets a second chance. Or, rather, he makes it for himself. It is not a chance of reconciliation or of love—that is too late—but of acting with moral courage and of asserting his will to the full—when he's old enough to command with authority in any case.

The Gerald Middletons, the liberal humanists of the professional class, with their nineteenth-century inheritance, have been the victims of a good deal of sceptical inquiry since the Thirties. They have been made symbolic figures, sometimes satirically, sometimes tragically, of a fundamental error. Mr Wilson, I am glad to see, is more generous. He does not overencumber Gerald Middleton with symbolism nor does he overload him with historical responsibility. Middleton is a good man with resources still to use. Good men have these resources. As far as the novel is concerned he is an excellent figure for conducting us through forty years of English life, and among a large number of characters, with perspicacity. And here lies the great originality of Mr Wilson as a novelist and the richness of his book. Its moral seriousness is matched by the comic explosions in our traditions. We are not Puritans: we are ironists. We can take a blow on the chin without hysteria. We see old Rose Lorimer boring a monkish academic audience with her well-known theories—she has gone off the rails of scholarship into the wilderness of the 'wider view'—we see the angry Professor Clun taking his academic disappointments out on his shrinking wife, with the sadism of a Casaubon. We see one of Middleton's sons, inheriting his mother's sentimentality, a self-deceived Radical with an act and a radio celebrity, in all the comedy of the sincerely insincere. We see his uneasy homosexual life, his awful young men. There is the sloppy yet generous Rammage who runs a boarding-house for these derelicts. There is Mrs Salad, Middleton's salacious and Dickensian housekeeper who is sentimental about his love nest. With sly, Cockney hypocrisy, she knows perfectly well what her son Vin and his boy friend, Larrie, are up to, and she lapses into a little shop-lifting herself—with plenty of tears when she is caught. And then, more respectable than these character parts and more subtle, there are Middleton's cloying and sentimental Danish wife, his raffish, twentyish mistress, Dolly, who is 'all on her ownio' and cannot keep off the bottle —she is cured by a gush of British Empire feeling in the Second World War and becomes deliciously prim in old age. In the younger generation there is her successor, the arty, hard-swearing Bohemian wench, Elvira—another hockey-playing Britannia gone wrong—full of candour but also full of gin; and, best of all, there is young Robin Middleton's French wife. Her grim conventionality, her avarice, her family egotism, her narrow mind and her dry resistance to moral inquiry are the answer to the Anglo-Saxon madness. For her, the whole trite meaning of existence is in the military certainties of family life, its boring seniorities, its day-dreams of successful lawsuits with in-laws. Her husband's (Anglo-Saxon) response is 'to use sincerity as his only protest against her existence'. By which matriarch shall we be ruled? By the knuckle-raps of a cynical French bourgeoise or by the fey and whimsical Dane, with her trolls, her gluttony and her humourless 'little mutter-ism'? Shall we be pickled in vinegar or suffocated by eiderdowns? Looking at her sons, the wife of the elusive English exogamist 'regarded their quarrels as a sort of tribute to her—with more truth than she realized'. She had the 'graciousness one expects of royalty and perhaps a little of their nullity'. She is a killer and a good cook. Young pansies love her and who knows that she does not know why?

Such a collection of characters is promising, especially when they are vividly realized and morally involved. Angus Wilson understands this and dives into their lives with alacrity and intelligence and sympathy. He is garrulous and epigrammatic but he moves quickly and at the right moment from person to person. The novel is closely patterned; indeed, one of its great pleasures is in its construction. But he is all effusive personality as a novelist, filling out his characters by opinionating and also, of course, taking from them some of their autonomy in so doing. In this he is like D. H. Lawrence and not like George Eliot, our great dutymonger. He has no great care for style, is more for English truculence than English urbanity. He is wicked in epigram though less sharp in his satire in this novel than he was in his short stories. He succeeds in the portrayal of character, is rather parsimonious of scenes (there is more opinionating reminiscence and talk). There are one or two very good scenes, of course. The ghastly party at the end of the book contains some delightful culture snobbery; the happy family dinner which is broken up when Dolly gets drunk is wonderful, surprising and rather moving. And any place where Larrie the Irish spiv turns up is packed with interest. Larrie and Vin are masterpieces of original observation and though I don't care for the melodramatic motor accident—a very odd fantasy to occur to a writer so on the spot as Mr Wilson—the whole business of Larrie's hysteria is absorbingly done.

In every generation one or two novelists revise the conventional picture of English character. Mr Wilson does this. There was morbidity, madness, even sourness in his stories—precisely qualities which our sociable tradition eschewed. They needed to be introduced by someone with humanity. We needed to recover our broadness without losing our moral sense. He has also bedded out in our rank social soil some of the hot-house blooms of our Dickensian tradition. Mrs Salad, for example, is a perennial London joy:

'Now the cyclermums is as delicate as my sister's skin. Her husband wouldn't have her wear a soiled garment not a day longer than was needed. Spurgins Tabernacle they was.'

This poetic old dear is nastier than Mrs Gamp, for she is close to crime and is thoroughly shady. She was—she is—a lavatory attendant and no shame to her; but that is a life, not a fantasy. Mr Wilson is subtle in conveying the social foundations of egocentricity. Mrs Salad is not a middle-class joke. He has given his people moral natures. He sees England with what looks like a foreign eye. That, for me, is an important virtue in a novel which, in any case, impresses by its range and its power of re-stating issues.

*　　*　　*

When we move on to a later novel, *No Laughing Matter*, we see what Mr Wilson owes to the histrionic tradition which goes back to Fielding and came to full bloom in Dickens. If Mr Wilson continues to be an anthropologist at work among the remnant of the upper middle class, he sees this class as people to whom performance is second nature. Whatever their virtues, their vices, their successes or their disasters, they carry them onto the stage, and can even be said to avoid self-knowledge by exposing themselves. One reviewer has correctly stated that Mr Wilson's perceptions here come from his gifts of mimicry and ventriloquism.

The period of *No Laughing Matter* lies between about 1911 and 1960 and we first see the whole Matthews family through the veil of their several daydreams. They are creating imaginary selves as they sit watching an early Wild West film. To only one of them, Great Aunt Rickard—known as Mouse—might the real Wild West conceivably have been known. The classic English spinster—she wanders about with a parrot on her shoulder and a sharp rat-a-tat-tat of sarcasms on her tongue—she has been a lonely, intrepid nomad. She has been at home in deserts, wild mountains, Indian and Asiatic plains. The rest of the family are sodden in unrealized fantasy. Billy Pop, the father—clever of Mr Wilson to hit upon the moment when Americanisms first came to England—is a failed writer of the Savoy and Strand period, a lazy, boozy philanderer living on the money of his wife's family. His jokes are terrible; his philosophizings evasive; he decays happily into shabby, Bohemian dandyism. The mother, mockingly known as the Countess by her bright and hostile children, is an Edwardian snob with a false accent—she says 'beautah' for 'beauty', 'meh' for 'me'. She lives in dreams of second-rate social grandeur, is capricious, petulant, very randy and rather unclean. Her taste in lovers is coarse. Her husband goes in for tarts. She can't afford the large Kensington house they all live in, on the grandparents' money, where all the cooking and cleaning is done by an old, fighting Cockney woman—who, in a pseudo-upper-class family, has a happy life as a knockabout comedian with a richly dirty mind. Her position gives her huge histrionic gifts a chance. Here she is, rolling home drunk:

Half past two. And down the road she comes. With a too ral, too ral, aye, does your ma know you're out? Swing, swing, how the bleeding pavements swing. Steady, me little cock sparrer. Hold on to the railing. Whoops, she goes! All to feed the fishes. Christ, what's that? There he comes, my own little Bobby, swinging his truncheon. . . . What about it, cock, lend us the end of your finger? But they wouldn't lend you a sausage, not one of them, the bleeders. Not if your name *was* Henrietta Stoker, mother unknown, probably titled, six years with the Honourable Mrs Pitditch-Perkins, French cooking trained by Monser Jools what had been at the Savoy. Oh, Lord, up she comes. Oh, Jesus help me. . . . Treated like dirt by the lot of them. Reagen do this, Reagen do that. Lend us a quid. Reagen. My name's Henrietta I'll thank you. . . . Tradesmen owed everywhere, the guv'nor boozed every night and SHE can't keep her legs shut. . . . Regular old cockney I am and one of the family. Make them laugh a caution sometimes. Oh, Ria she's a toff, darn't she look immensikoff, and they all shouted, waatch Ria!

The children of this quarrelling, sour-smelling setup are gifted and wretched. They see themselves as actors in a broken-down, stranded Rep company; and when things get bad they play what is called The Game. In this they act out a court scene in which the awful parents are on mock trial. Their satire is bitchy and disabused yet it is also compassionate. Why did whimsical Billy Pop call his wife The Countess? It's a nursery genteelism for Cuntess. Marcus, one of the sons, who will become a homosexual later in the chronicle, plays the part of his loved and hated mother:

'Do you remember, Billah,' she asked, 'when we bunnah hugged till dawn? Your breath smells Billah. Oh God! You've let yourself go to pieces.' 'Come to that,' says Billy Pop [played by Rupert who will eventually become a famous actor]. 'Come to that you stink like a whore's knocking shop.'

Quentin, the eldest son, home from the 1914 war, plays the judge all his life. He will eventually become a left-wing journalist, a trouble to the Communists and Socialists in the Spanish war. He will be beaten up by Irish Black Shirts, refuse to sign a manifesto in Moscow, and will end up as a well-known national broadcaster. He is never ridiculed, though he is often shouted down; if he acts it is in the real world and represents Mr Wilson's committal and conscience. (But public speaking is a form of acting.) Look at the others. Honest, clumsy Gladys, tennis player, first to know as a child what Cuntess means, and shamed by the semi-bankruptcy of the family, becomes a business girl and is eventually the secretive mistress of an obvious crook called Alf whose commercial affairs are sweaty-faced fraud. Naturally, he lands her in jail in order to save his own skin. The actress in Gladys emerges when she appears in court; she skilfully hides Alf's identity by behaving frivolously and impudently to the Judge. There is an important point of character here; it amounts to a social diagnosis too: the family has no respect for society. The hated family binds them. Gladys is a clumsy E. M. Forsterite who puts 'personal relationships' first, even bad ones. After four years in jail she settles down with an easy-going 'bloke' and breeds dogs.

Then there are Margaret and Sukey. Margaret will turn into a writer of integrity, waspish to begin with, softer and popular later on. We read bits of the novels she is writing and her progress is expertly and seriously shown. *Her* acting is seen in her compulsion to turn the family reality into the unreality of literature. Sukey, a headmaster's wife and practical mother, seems totally without inner life, but her energies go on to a stage where self-preservation and duty are in conflict. Easily settled: Sukey elects, *à l'anglaise*, for the great escape called Worry. Marcus, the youngest, whose schoolboy scenes with his brother are very well done, spits in the face of one of his mother's lovers, turns homosexual and, imitating mother, invites his boyfriends to the house. There is a very funny bedroom scene with a Colonel who combines disciplinary moral lectures with seduction. Eventually Marcus finds the right man and goes in for lavish, theatrical parties in Hampstead and selling modern paintings. The thing to note is that all these children of the decadence are iron-willed. They have gone through a dreadful family mill; it has hardened their egos, and if they are emotionally disjointed they are not emotionally dead or deceived.

These are the people who have somehow to find their way through the Twenties and to react to the rise of Fascism, the Communist revival, the Second World War; to changes of fashion, to political and literary meetings. Quentin has to fight against being called a crank. Margaret, the novelist, has to defend herself against the charge that she is indifferent to the people she writes about—and indeed a lot of Mr Wilson's very witty book, which is full of malice as well as ideas, is a defence of the view that malice is not alien to the passions for truth, integrity, and the affections: a lot of blah and stupidity has to be cauterized. The picture of Margaret thinking her pernickety way from the real life character before her into the imaginary relations she is creating is good. In fact all the characters are sound in talk and action for—as one knows from his short stories—Mr Wilson is a master of the small iceberg that has much meaning beneath it. We see Rupert—who will be a success in Chekhov—studying his part seriously, and here the theatre scenes are excellent. The moment when Rupert gambles and astutely seduces a great actress is very good too. There are many such sharp instances within the cinematic commentary that carries the chronicle forward. And the characters are not static. They change with the years. Even the hopeless parents, Billy Pop and the Countess, now supported by the family, become more tolerable as their joints stiffen. They have a cock-eyed dignity. Billy Pop's literary memoirs, recalling the good old days when he wrote that series on cricket for *Blackwoods*, are beautifully parodied.

Mr Wilson is a wit who repairs the damage he does by the

natural overflow of his talent. He inclines to have too many ideas and in this novel his stress on The Game played by the family seems to me excessive. It is true that game-playing is a common escapist device in the lives of the people he is describing, but since all the characters in this novel are seen on their inner stage, it is overdoing the matter to repeat it in a family charade. Another difficulty is that the Matthewses are a special case: as Bohemians they are cut off from the rest of society, they are seen in almost picturesque isolation: we see remarkably little of their lovers and friends or the society from which these outsiders come. And finally, when a younger generation appears, they seem pale, unformed, even exhausted when compared with their shameless forbears. It is an occupational risk of the novelist who is writing a chronicle that he will tend, in the end, to become more intent on the years than on his characters.

HENRY GREEN

In the Echo Chamber

LOOKING BACK ON the novels of the late Twenties, a period
when style and originality counted above all, I still think
Henry Green showed a startling certainty of direction in his
first novel. *Blindness* was written when he was about eighteen:
superficially autobiographical, it was only very slightly deriva-
tive. The remarkable quality was the young author's accomplished sense of his 'line': he would sacrifice everything to
seeing and hearing, not as a reporter, but as an artist feeling his
way into the consciousness of others. Random calamity was to
have a marked place in Henry Green's mature work and often
echoes the accidental skids of our garrulous minds; but when,
in this first book, the youthful writer is accidentally blinded
for life, Green was not so much interested in blindness as a case
for pity or stoicism but as a device for intensifying his
sensibility and retrieving exact memory as a writer. Blindness
was to be a journey into a country otherwise lost. The subject
of all Henry Green's later novels is the inner language and
landscape in which his characters lead their real lives. Under
the spoken rigmarole they conceal their resourcefulness as
human beings.

When he came to write his masterpieces, *Living, Caught* and
Loving, his characters were for the most part ordinary workers
on the factory floor, firemen, stunned soldiers, dull people in
offices, servants and (occasionally) frantic upper-class people.
The striking thing is that this distinctly upper-class artist is
pretty well the first English novelist to have listened to work-
ing-class speech and to have understood its overtones and
undertones, without being what, in the Thirties, one would

have called politically committed. The 'committed' novelists did nothing like as well. He could, of course, have been playing a clever game; but he was not. The morbid, the comic, the lyrical and even the mannered aspects of his talent were not affected: fierce, fantastic and eccentric as it could be, his material came from the outside and mingled with his nature. He was not in the least sentimental: his eye was hard, his ear sharp. Some very fine artists impose themselves, but Henry Green belonged to those who masochistically seek to let their characters speak through them. In so speaking, they may expose more than they know; but don't we all stubbornly feel that, for better or worse, we are more than we know? There is a muddled justification for our existence. We are encrusted in something like a private culture.

In *Blindness*, we are first shown the boy before his accident. Precocious, scornfully determined to be a great writer, and with a quick, educated mind, he is quite certain to be talented. He is also rich. His short diary about friends and quarrels at a great Public School is packed with swank and tetchiness. Then the accident occurs. He is reduced at once to helplessness in the family's grand country house, to be petted and pitied by the servants and to arouse guilt in his stepmother, a hard-riding, capable ruler of the estate and the village; she is struggling between her sense of emotional inadequacy and her natural, ruthless worldliness. The boy's blindness—as he coldly notes—has provided the household with an emotional orgy, enlarging dramas of pity and bustling self-importance. In the stepmother's chattering mind we see the beginnings of Henry Green's gift for drawing on the inexhaustible wells of human egoism.

She leaves her dining room for the sitting room which looks out onto a rose garden:

It ought to look well this year, not that he would see it, though. She had lots of things to do this morning, she would not let the thing come up and crush her. His was the sort of nature which needed to be left alone, so it was no use going to see him. Plans must be made for when his new life would begin, and some idea might emerge out of her work. Being blind he could do work for the other blind and so not feel solitary, but get the feeling of a Regiment. Meanwhile there was the Nursing Association. She must write to his friends, too, they ought to know that he was blind. Would they really care? But, of course, anyone who knew John must care. Then their letters would come in return, shy and halting, with a whole flood of consolation from the neighbours, half of whom did not care in the least. She would have to answer them: but no, she couldn't. Then they would say that the blow had aged her, she had said that so often herself. Their letters would be full of their own little griefs, a child who had a cold, a husband worried by his Indian liver, one who had been cut publicly by Mrs So-and-So—but this wasn't fair. They would write rather of someone of theirs who had died recently or years and years ago. And she would answer suitably, for of course by now one knew what to say, but it was hateful people laying little private bits of themselves bare and she being expected to do likewise. Still, it would be all over some day.

She took up the Nursing Accounts.

A whole fox-hunting society, at a time when the big houses are beginning to go, comes to life, and is at a loss to know how to feel. For the boy, the new life means a proud angry battle with self-pity, an intensifying of the will to remember every detail of the country: exactly what the fields looked like, how the fish rose in the stream, where the grass and the nettles met, understanding sounds, listening to the inflexions of voices, wincing at too much oozing sentiment, discriminating between the notes of truth and untruth. The incipient ruthlessness of the artist is strengthened. There follows a halting friendship with the ragged daughter of the local, unfrocked, gin-soaking clergyman, a girl humiliated by her father's dilapidation. This episode is a shade too bizarre in a Powys-y rural manner, but the halting talk between the shy, rather cruel boy and the straightforward, kind girl is excellent and shows us the start of Green's remarkable talent for drawing simple young women. His gift lies in conveying the strangeness of the un-spoken that underlies the spoken and for real dialogue which is a juxtaposition of voices that do not answer each other, but continue lives that will come nearer and will, in the end, be separate. Being young is a quest.

In the last stage of the boy's friendship with the girl, one sees Green's own mind made up as a writer. Country life is sinister, childish, futile. Towns and cities where real people work at their machines are to be his world, among people who have reserves of direction and skill, where humanity exists and love is grown-up. At the end of the book the out-of-date country house is sold. The boy and his stepmother go to London and there is new incitement to make what he can of life.

Like most first novels of talent, *Blindness* is a book of striking pages rather than a sound whole. The leap forward to the factory life of his next book, *Living*, is enormous. The study of blindness seems to express a strain of morbidity which was valuable to Green because it was not sentimental; it was, rather, a way of unselfing himself in order to enter the maze in which the minds and feelings and interests of ordinary people, totally foreign to himself, were going round and round in circles. He was not taking them up as a cause; he loved their mystery. He was a far closer and more feeling observer here than George Orwell was, for he had no polemic. Henry Green loved the obstinacy, the strangeness, the monotone of the deeply emotional culture which ran alongside his own cool one. Human repetitiousness was a sort of poetry for him. It also defined the inner territory of obscure rights, wrongs and blind stubbornness to which our devious self-interest or our waywardness clings like creeper. His people are new on top but old underneath. In spite of the mannerisms and a wild delight in calamity, Green seems to me to have been the most luminous novelist of the Thirties and Forties—as *Blindness* foretold—and truly seminal. For him people were echoing chambers. One has to pick out this voice or that before it turns into the general reverberation in which a society sinks its life.

HENRY JAMES

Birth of a Hermaphrodite

WHEN THE SECOND volume of Leon Edel's life of Henry James opens, the novelist is twenty-seven. He is forty by the end, a success, 'sufficiently great', but not yet the Master. The clever book-reviewer, the nimble writer of travel sketches, is at first seen worried and restive in Boston after his 'passionate pilgrimage' in Europe, fussed by the choice between American virtue and the beautiful European corruption. (In a hundred years how *that* international moral tale has changed!) He goes to his native New York and slaves for a while as a high-class hack. Travel writing once more releases him for Italy, France, Switzerland and Turgenev's Baden, but by the time he is thirty-three, his pleasant job as sentimental traveller for the *New York Tribune* is ending and he has run through the flimsy, seasonal acquaintance of his fellow expatriates in the spas and capitals. France has disappointed in the end for he has 'seen all round' Flaubert and Zola; French social life has turned out (it always does to the foreigner) to be impenetrable. He has been thrown upon the boulevards among a lot of third-rate tourists.

Sooner or later any travelling American swallows his love-hate for the British and is subdued by the convenience of the English tongue. The strain of linguistics gives place to the pleasure of even vulgar conversation. So James comes to London and finds what he needs—tradition, the back numbers of *Punch*, speaking likenesses of Dickens's people and Thackeray's everywhere, coal fires, draughts, and a home. Looking out of his window off Piccadilly he reflects that Becky Sharp once lived round the corner in Curzon Street and that—sublime contentment—Lord Ashburton's dirty brown brick wall is across the way. James was a Londoner at last, yet not quite smoked and kippered to our condition. He indeed fell back on French in his happiness: *'Je suis absolument comme chez moi.'* The phrase preserves a nuance in his philandering relation to the city and the country he was, in the end, to adopt.

There was never anything flighty in Henry James's movements. He came to London with a prepared campaign and an inner calendar in his head. He steamed ponderously in like an engine, on time. If there is one thing that both Leon Edel's volumes have brought out it is that the Master was a major strategist as a writer and in his social life. There is—or was—no more highly-trained snob than the Boston snob; he got onto the right people at once and, that done, London was easy to penetrate, for the right people were not sticklers and asked only to be amused. Their deplorable lack of 'analytical intellect' assured that they would be pleasant. London was the chosen site, a 'regular basis of mundane existence', for James's next battle: after success, the organized achievement of Greatness.

Our usual picture of James comes from the later, old Pretender period when he seems to be genuflecting, somewhere in space, before the image of Art, mysteriously sustained by an invisible private income. The young James with the glossy beard is quite a different person: dashing, shrewd about ways and means, burning with energy. There is vast confidence in his malice and his ironic laughter. He is absolutely professional. He delights to earn his living; he is tough with editors; he is prompt and clever with his pot-boilers; he has an eye to serials and commissions. He was long-headed enough to know, within six months, when he would be able to switch to greatness. He arrived in London for the publication of a work of serious criticism and of his early novels, which were unknown here. A few rapid moves and he knew everyone. At first agog, but soon he was in the clubs—a 'member' in the full, soporific sense. A word from Henry Adams—the supreme

Yankee snob and expert at the game—and he was staying in the best houses. The lazy, genial Thackeray had been ruined by dining out; for James it was part of the plan. In his second winter, he had dined out 140 times and in the best society—'behold me after dinner conversing affably with Mr Gladstone.' Not always, of course, in the best. There were flops. There were shabby, literary ladies. There were dreary Oxfordish parties, shoppish and local in their eternal gossip. If he was bowled over by the handsomeness of English men they had, he noticed, dirty hands.

Handsome himself, witty, attentive to women, especially to old ladies, James was enormously popular in mid-Victorian London. His talk was light yet serious. He pleased everyone, though he was careful not to speak his mind outright. The curse laid upon the British—it was the complaint of Taine— was their lack of that analytical mind. He never really got to the heart of the English matter. Privileged travellers, like James, tend to see any society as obligingly static and displaying the end-products of character: to the forces that make a people what they are, James was blind. It is not the business of the novelist to do so, but the novels of Henry James tell us little about *English* life beyond the relations of the rich to their servants.

There are, all the same, two Henry Jameses: the novelist with his 'beautiful contrivances' and exquisite adumbrations who confines himself, with one or two exceptions, to upper-class life; and the traveller who slums with any company. He mooched in the London streets, swallowed the fog, looked at the gin-soaked squalor and so far unbuttoned as to go off with the crowd to the Derby. An unsuspected England showed itself—violent, jolly and uninhibited. He had, on the whole, a low opinion of the British female, though admittedly she did not run, after an early blossoming, to the American stringiness. The British female of the lower orders was alarming. She was 'too stout, too hot, too red, too thirsty, too boisterous, too strangely accoutred', yet (one was obliged to add) 'useful, robust and prolific'. Like Britannia, in short. In *The Princess Casamassima* he turned her to account in the fine picture of Millicent Henning, with her Cockney beauty, 'her bad grammar and good health ... her shrewd perceptions and grotesque opinions'. (James could not bear it that English women were healthy.)

Once more in this second volume Leon Edel gracefully disposes of the notion that quiet lives, and especially the lives of writers, are uninteresting. James toiled. The hours of his life are filled up less with minutes than with words. They edge him out, phrase by phrase, from nearly all external experience except eating, flirting, walking alone at night and sleeping. The clues to the inner dramas are in his work. James's inner life—perhaps this is true of all novelists—is an affair of ghosts. The figures of father, mother and above all of William the brother and rival actively haunt him and provide their crises. No doubt all families are tyrannies of the affections, but the James family, withdrawn on principle from the contagion of participation in American life, conscientiously standing for 'being' rather than 'doing', was like some closed city state. The mother—'too sacred' to be described by James—ruled it in what we now accept as the American habit. To think of breaking with it meant, in William's case and that of his sister, invoking the protection of illness. They are all held together by brilliance, irony, the private devices. William cannot manage to marry until he is thirty-six and is, strangely, in Europe when his child is born. Henry escapes because he is the spoiled boy, the second son, Angel as he was mockingly called, hiding his forbidding will to power and his egotism behind the mask of meekness. His deepest friendships are with elderly women, although there is one episode—his presumably platonic and prolonged and rather secret flirtation with Constance Fennimore Woolson—in which, meaning to be merely disturbing, he was himself disturbed and challenged. It led to headaches and, later, to the refinements of remorse. In art and the egotism of the artist James had found his safety and liberation.

But the ghosts could suddenly play a decisive part. They can be seen grouping and regrouping in the early stories where William and Henry grapple in disguise. When William got married the profound relation of Henry with his brother was shaken, and Mr Edel notes that one of his worst stories, *Confidence*, was written at this time: two young men fall for the same young woman who is called, of all things, Angela! The Angel has feminized himself. This might have been a fantasy of passing interest but the fraternal crisis coincided with the uproar in America about his study of Hawthorne: his deepest feelings were stirred.

Henry James, conquering London and its literary world, could be as assertive and powerful as Christopher Newman; but rejected like Newman—or pushed to the wall by his elder brother—told that he wasn't fit to play with rough boys or that his writing was full of knots and bows and ribbons, found himself reminded forcibly that he was a perpetual 'mere junior'.

Until now his novels had been about heroes. In the one seeming exception, *Daisy Miller*, the girl is seen through the eyes of a man. Henceforth they would be about heroines responding 'to their destinies in a world that jilted, denied and betrayed'. He would write *Washington Square* and *The Portrait of a Lady*. Was this a matter of imaginative dexterity, or did it come from his nature? A hermaphrodite—according to Mr Edel—discovered himself.

And in *The Portrait* Mr Edel directs us, with great perspicacity, to one of those inner dramas of compensation and confident self-extending that bring a writer's powers to maturity—if they come at the right time. Who is Osmond in *The Portrait*? He is, Mr Edel says, the hidden side of James himself, when his snobbery prevailed over his humanity and arrogance and egotism over his urbanity and his benign view of the human comedy . . . in creating him Henry put into him his highest ambition and drive to power—the grandiose way in which he confronted his destiny. . . . In the hands of a limited being, like Osmond, the drive to power ended in dilettantism and petty rages. In Henry's hands the same drive had given him unbounded creativity.

If he closely watches the ghosts in James's life, Mr Edel is not tempted into those murkier areas of the psychological limbo which have been irresistible to the reckless school of biography. We are shown James living as we might have seen him. There he goes riding every morning in the Campagna with some lady he has charmed; there he goes out for his night walks in London; there he sits reading at the Reform; watching, very shocked, the great Turgenev playing with Pauline Viardot's children on the floor; obdurately working all the afternoon in Italy while William waits impatiently for him to finish. James lived in the extremes of solitude and sociability; his is one of the most peopled lives lived by a man of genius, for the genius depended on their chatter. To have got all these people back out of literature into James's life as Mr Edel has done is remarkable in itself, but the skill with which these things are made to build up James's own life as a man is more remarkable. The short chapters each carefully pointed, take one with alacrity along the crowded peregrinations of James's mind and person, without a moment's boredom. Mr Edel has come close to the excited spontaneous sensibility and intelligence of a man who baffles us by being enormous and yet who, in a way almost enviable, has no life at all.

★   ★   ★

By the time the fourth volume of Leon Eidel's rich and searching biography of Henry James opens, the Master has had to
face the shattering fact of the suicide of Miss Woolson in
Venice, and is about to receive another blow in the very sanc-
tum of his so far invulnerable egotism: in his art. His plots for
success in the theatre (and as an operator James was as exhaustive here as he was in his social stratagems), his hopes of the
financial magnificence of the best-sellers at a moment when he
was himself becoming noticeably less saleable, are to be
brutally dashed by the booing of *Guy Domville*. He took the
affair as if his person had been assaulted, as if he had been
mugged. The strategist, in life and in art, the addict of military
memoirs, has had a public defeat, and at a truly 'awkward
age'. He is fifty; a younger irreverent generation of realists,
who have no interest in High Romance, has burst open the
door. He is called further to account by his first humiliating
attack of gout.

The next five years, in Mr Edel's diagnosis, are a period of
'nervous breakdown', and he is to be shown slowly emerging
from it by his invincible belief in the therapy of his art. At his
age many artists turn to easier remedies, or slacken in their
vigilance, for even art has its temptations; but James (perhaps
because he was a solitary and a man of puritan energy) had
always known that the important thing was to increase difficulty. In his case—and I would have said for all—the
temptation is to thin oneself by looking forward: the difficult
task is to reconstitute oneself by looking back. And so Mr
Edel's purpose is to show James performing on himself 'what
Freud was busily demonstrating'—the power to heal oneself
of hardening wounds by retreat to earliest experience. The
process is dramatically clear: it is not a question of curing
himself by work, but of divining the right work. James found
it in the treacherous five years, by writing his tales of children,
ghosts and phantasmagoria: it is the period of *The Pupil*, *The
Awkward Age*, *What Maisie Knew*, *The Turn of the Screw* and of

that mystifying search for the heart of personality, *The Sacred Fount*, before the spacious final works are attempted.

For the comedy of Jamesian anecdote Professor Edel has little use. The adroit letters (he has said before) are either recklessly discharged smoke-screens or a collection of tactical feints. They are histrionically concealing. Professor Edel notes enough of James's familiar social life at Lamb House, his meetings with Kipling and Meredith, the devastating visits of Edith Wharton, the last journey to Italy, his bicycle rides and so on, to keep the spry, practical, restless 'character' alive and to preserve his engaging momentousness. But the cure is the thing and Professor Edel studies it, until it completes itself at the end of the book, with the tremendous sight of the Master shaving off his beard. But Professor Edel relies on James's clue: 'The artist is in every page of every book from which he sought so assiduously to eliminate himself.'

The difficulty here is to avoid theory or dogmatic assertion about the meaning of echoes, symbols and images, and I don't know any writer who is so free of the vices psychology has offered to biography as Professor Edel is. He is pertinacious, but tactful, gracious and tender; indeed, this is the most moving of his four volumes. His suggestions, gathered from the novels, tend to build up a whole rather than a schematic figure, and he is aware that a writer may go far back into his past for a word or a crucial incident without consciously displaying an item of personal history. We can see Professor Edel's method at work in what he has to say about the melodramatic ending of *The Spoils of Poynton* and its possible relation to James's horrifying experience when he was booed off the stage after *Guy Domville*. Professor Edel notes that the book does not have one of James's traditional endings: why melodrama?

Perhaps because he had himself been forced to the centre of the stage, in a bit of melodrama not of his own making. His imagery went further back however than the recent disaster in

the St James's. In describing Mrs Gereth's departure from
Poynton and her loss of her antiques, *her* work of art, James
wrote 'the amputation had been performed. Her leg had come
off—she had now begun to stump along with the lovely
wooden substitute and would stump for life, and what her
young friend was to come and admire was the beauty of her
movement. . . .' Thus James had recourse in this work to one of
the most personal images out of his own childhood. It
suggests how vivid for all his life time was the memory of his
father's amputation and 'the noise . . . about the house'. The
father had lost his leg in a stable fire and Henry subsequently
had suffered a back injury while helping to fight a stable fire at
Newport. Amputation and fire: these symbols out of the past
now forced themselves into the story he was telling. Poynton
and its 'spoils' had to be destroyed as *Guy Domville* was
destroyed.

One practical result of the failure in the theatre was that he
now turned to planning his stories as scenarios. This unluckily
doubled their length. We are at the beginning of the period
when over and over again his stories are too long for their
subject. (This is true, for the contemporary reader, of masterpieces like *The Pupil*.) Before, he never revised; now he will
revise interminably; and when he takes up dictation, the
manner will take on the appearance of an intricate private
reverie.

So the cure has its price. But the gains are extraordinary in
life and in literature. By taking his mind back to childhood,
James was obliged to consider his femininity. His masculinity
had been driven underground.

To be male was to risk [in the remote fantasy of childhood]
such things as amputation like his father; . . . he could escape
by thinking himself a little girl.

The rivalry with the older male, William, appears in tale after tale in many forms. Lack of male conviction was the weakness of *Guy Domville*. In retreating to Lamb House and brooding on his past, James was retreating into a simulacrum of his life in the James family; and hence the buried struggles of childhood come to the surface. The feelings that arose out of the past were a 'kind of conscious nightmare'. In *The Turn of the Screw* the ghosts are the ghosts of his boyhood. Little Miles's 'rude' battle with the governess, telling her he doesn't want to be cooped up with females, is a transference of James's own conflict. Miles is defeated, and it is important to see that, told in the first person by the governess, the story is a statement of female hysteria. The femininity of Henry James is speaking. Maisie is a study of himself in boyhood—she is, I remember noting years ago, facetiously addressed as 'my dear sir' by one of her guardians. Nanda of *The Awkward Age* would be a projection of the Henry of late adolescence. The little girls—and without writing a conscious series (as Professor Edel shows) James studies them at progressive ages—emerge 'out of the personal healing' which was going on under the surface of the practical, ambitious, successful man of the world.

Professor Edel's patient and careful method makes his point; for although one can say that any author's life is buried in his work in this way, James's distinction is that he knew what he was doing: his father's faith in compensations was part of family training. Only occasionally does the reliance on verbal echoes seem to me strained. When the governess feels her 'blow in the stomach' it seems merely ingenious to trace this back to the blow in the stomach James said he had had at the St James's Theatre. And when the child Effie is murdered by drowning, I think Professor Edel is pushing matters when he links this with what James called his 'subaqueous' feelings after *Guy Domville*.

The final chapters of the volume are as moving and perceptive as those that were given to the story of Miss Woolson in the earlier volume. There, a hardness of heart and a good deal of disingenuousness appeared in James's character. He certainly feared entanglement, but the part played by a distaste that looks secretive and snobbish seems plain. That by dying our friends extinguish part of ourselves is true enough, and it is characteristic of James's truth-telling and glacial egotism to show this as an affront. In *The Beast in the Jungle* he knows remorse. The present volume contains an account of James suffering as Miss Woolson suffered, in his extraordinary passion for the young, crude and climbing Norwegian sculptor Hendrik Andersen. They saw little of each other, but the separations were agonizing and the letters are filled not only with ironical advice to the young god who was vulgarly on the make, but with physical longings. He wanted to touch the young man. He wanted to hug and embrace him: 'lean on me as a brother and a lover'. And 'I hold you close' and 'I feel my arms around you'. These expressions may be simply a well-known mode of Victorian emotionalism:

> Allowances must be made [Professor Edel says] for James's long puritan years, the confirmed habits of denial, the bachelor existence, in which erotic feeling had been channelled into hours of strenuous work and the wooing of *mon bon*. One also must remember that James had a fear of loss of masculinity . . . James was constitutionally incapable of belonging to the underworld of sex into which Oscar Wilde had drifted.

His feelings had been transferred to the intellect. His philanderings with his many women friends went to fanciful lengths, and were really utterances of High Romance. But clearly, this time, there was passion on James's part. He was still writing it at the age of seventy. He comes out of the affair with his reply to another young man who had asked him what port he had set out from as a novelist:

> The port from which I set out was, I think, that of the *essential loneliness of my life*—and it seems to me the port, in sooth, to

which again finally my course directs itself. This loneliness [since I mention it!]—what is it still but the deepest thing about one? Deeper about me, at any rate, than anything else, deeper than my 'genius', deeper than my 'discipline', deeper than any pride, deeper above all, than the deep counter-minings of art.

He wrote this while correcting the proofs of *The Sacred Fount*—that baffling and even trivial book which Professor Edel sees as the final therapeutic act that would mark his self-healing. Until now, as a novelist, he had never dealt with love in his novels, except as a 'force destructive of—or in competition with—power and aesthetic beauty'. He had now discovered that his egotism was vulnerable. Professor Edel's *Life* has not only scope and mastery of lively detail and argument; it goes with bold and yet controlled insight into the labyrinth of a great creative imagination. The man and the artist have been joined—a feat that biography so rarely succeeds in.

* * *

Henry James's *The American Scene* is still one of the very few excellent books of travel by an American about his own country. He is as exact and prophetic in his own restricted way as the extraordinary and very different Tocqueville was in his. The book is unique in a genre where—strangely enough, among a foot-loose people—American literature is very poor; for penetrating observation and evocation of the land and the cities we have to turn to novels and, above all, poetry. The remarkable thing about the book is that although it was written in 1905, and in spite of the huge changes that have occurred in America since that time, it presents (as Leon Edel says in a troubled introduction) an essential America that is still recognizable.

This ought not to surprise us: great artists are always far-seeing. They easily avoid the big stumbling blocks of fact.

They rely on their own simplicity and vision. It is fact-fetich-ism that has given us those scores and scores of American books on America, the works of sociologists, anthropologists, topical 'problem' hunters, working-parties and statisticians, which in the end leave us empty. Henry James succeeds because he rejects information. He was himself the only information he required.

It should be unfailingly proved against me that my opportunity found me incapable of imparting information, incapable alike of receiving and imparting it; for then, and then only, would it be clearly attested that I *had* cared and understood.

He was looking for a personal relationship to the scene he had left twenty years before. In so many other books on the country the sense of a relation is lacking; indeed, they leave one with an impression of a lonely continent, uncontemplated, unloved, unfelt by a people who have got so much out of it, as they move on, that they see little in it and give or leave nothing of themselves to the scene. How else to explain that sensation of things, places, even people abandoned which is so painful in the American landscape! How often one has felt what James sensed about certain American scenes, especially in New England:

And that was doubtless, for the story seeker, absolutely the story: the constituted blankness was the whole business, and one's opportunity was all, thereby, for a study of exquisite emptiness.

Or:

Charming places, charming objects, languish all round, under designations that seem to leave on them the smudge of a great vulgar thumb—which is precisely a part of the pleading land appears to hint to you when it murmurs, in autumn, its intelligent refrain. If it feels itself better than so many phases of its fate, so there are spots where you see it turn up at you, under some familiar tasteless inflections of this order, the plaintive eye of a creature wounded with a poisoned arrow.

Henry James knew what the poison was. It would eventually wreck the American cities—a process our planners, always out of date, are eager to imitate in England today.

James was a traveller, that is to say, a story-seeker to the marrow. His novels themselves are conscious journeys into the interior. He had started by writing travel sketches of things in France, Italy and Germany and England when he was young; the 'vignettes' of a sentimental traveller, meant to tease the American fancy for the Atlantic trip. *The American Scene* is a totally different matter. Perhaps at the age of sixty the returning expatriate originally promised himself one more sentimental pilgrimage. But in twenty years American life had passed through a crucial change. It could either sink him or raise him by the challenge. He was roused. Half the pleasure of the book comes from the sight of a travelling mind reinvigorated. He met the challenge with a richer and revived analytical gift. He rejected the journalistic temptation. In the twenty years since 1883 a huge immigrant invasion had changed the character of the cities; big business, the great industrial monopolies, had taken total power and had imposed the business ethos; the pursuit of money had become the engulfing and only justifying role. New York had been a rough, low-built sea port with pigs rooting in the streets of lower Manhattan when he left, Central Park was a farmland. He returned to find all Manhattan crammed, and the skyscrapers rising—'simply the most piercing notes in that concert of the expensively provisional into which your supreme sense of New York resolves'.

James ignored the colossal news item. He saw that his subject was not shock and that he was not there to advertise or boost the obvious. His subject was how the consciousness of a half-repentant expatriate would be affected, and what inner meanings and sensibilities he could offer in return. Guilt there would be, but distaste: nostalgia for what was gone, but a feeling for the drama; he would have to be both personal and yet the analyst. He became the seeker. He would have to lay himself open to the full bewilderment of his situation. In his introduction to an earlier edition of this book, W. H. Auden described it as a prose poem; an excellent description. Generously evocative and labyrinthine in its tact, it also shows a man struggling with love and menace. The skyscrapers are a 'vocabulary of thrift' but there are 'uglier words' for that. With mild but deadly truth they evoke (he says)

the consciousness of the finite, the menaced, the essentially *invented* state [that] twinkles ever, to my perception, in the thousand glassy eyes of those giants of the market.

Again and again, he remarks on the 'pathos' of a civilization so exuberantly on the move, but bewildered in having to accept itself as temporary. Of the new rich he writes:

What had it been their idea to *do*, the good people . . . do that is, in affirming their wealth with such innocent emphasis and yet not at the same time affirming anything else.

They live in houses that have

the candid look of costing as much as they knew how. Unmistakably they all proclaimed it—they would have cost still more had the way but been shown to them; and, meanwhile, they added, as with one voice, they would take a fresh start as soon as ever it should be. 'We are only instalments, symbols, stop-gaps', they practically admitted, and with no shade of embarrassment: 'expensive we are, we have nothing to do with continuity, responsibility, transmission, and don't in the least care what becomes of us after we have served our present purpose'.

And the governing motive:

To make so much money that you won't, that you don't 'mind' anything.

Not, as it has turned out, the awful sight of American cities. If you do 'mind' you can easily become an un-American activity.

For James, America was 'dancing on the thin crust of a volcano'. In personal relationships

the most that was as yet accomplished . . . was the air of un-mitigated publicity, publicity as a condition, as a doom from which there could be no appeal.

There was the inability to communicate, which was not felt as a loss among the new immigrants, but rather as a gain; they had become American. James, the native, puts his finger on what often dismays the chatty European traveller in his casual contacts: the American chill.

To isolate James's hostile impressions as I have done or to quote his final denunciation of the reigning spirit of the time —a denunciation which did not appear in the first American edition—is to give a misleading impression of a book warm in feeling and rich in texture. Every page contains a picture or a phrase that will bring New York, Boston, the scrub forest of New Hampshire, to the eyes, but backed by his long loving knowledge of the places. He records such deeply American things as allowing the forest to come down to the edges of the innumerable lakes. The story seeker, as he calls himself, continually questions the landscape in relation to himself, and it is the self-questioning which is at the heart of his ability to create the scene in the superb chapter on New Hampshire. Why does it seem to be Arcadian? Why was he always brought back to the thought that the woods and rocks insist on referring themselves to the idyllic? Was it because they bore no burden of history? The thought charms him, but another thought makes him sceptical: perhaps he rhapsodized now, because in Europe he had been deprived

> to excess—that is for too long—of naturalism in quantity. Here it was in such quantity as one hadn't for years to deal with; and that might by itself be a luxury corrupting the judgment.

The irony is subtle; but hasn't James hit exactly upon what drifts through one's mind as one drives the scores of miles through the scrub, the brown rock and grey rock of New England, or stands by some clear cold pond in the woods—the lyrical and, at the same time, crushing quantity of Nature, stupefying the mind? How much the love of quantity, together with its inexorable, umbrageous detail, has meant to an American mind.

James spent about a year as a returned native. Business and immigration were the important themes, alien to him and to his natural nostalgias; no searching was needed as far as business was concerned. That hit one in the face. The immigrants were more difficult, but he took a lot of trouble to see what was happening on New York's lower East Side.

There, as a writer, he was as excited as he was disturbed by what would happen to the language, and to character. How long would the melting take? Then he went South, and any romantic hopes he had were pinched by wretched weather and the general shabbiness. He is still good, but he is better on native ground. He discovered that Washington was the place where, for once, men ruled the conversation. Outside of known, friendly haunts, he had been starved of two things in America: conversation—all that was offered was talk—and privacy. He hated the open interior of the American club and house. But if, inevitably, he harks back to the times when a home was not a house, when locality existed and the tycoons were unknown, if he denounces the new age and sees it will lead to worse, he is soundly American in admiring the drama of the situation and in his feeling for the extravagant.

The search for the story, the inturned Jamesian story, is at once pertinacious and very touching. He creates an America because he creates himself in relation to it. The book is a true work of travel because it is a collaboration and with a living country that scatters a myriad unanswered questions about 'as some monstrous unnatural mother might leave a family of unfathered infants on door steps or in waiting rooms'.

EDMUND WILSON

Towards Revolution

IN 1972 EDMUND WILSON'S *To the Finland Station* was re-issued with an introduction written by him about a year before. The book seems to me to have become crisper, in some mysterious way, in the long interval, to have moved away from the topical domestic hopes of his youth into the classic condition and to be Wilson's most enlarging work. I cannot think of any other American historical essay so fine in texture, in this century. What did Wilson himself think of it? He understood its roots in the agitations of the Thirties. Authors are usually their own exact critics:

> It is all too easy to idealize a social upheaval which takes place in some other country than one's own.... The remoteness of Russia from the West evidently made it even easier for American socialists and liberals to imagine that the Russian Revolution was to get rid of an oppressive past, to scrap a commercial civilization, and to found, as Trotsky prophesied, the first really human society. We were very naïve about this. We did not foresee that the new Russia must contain a good deal of the old Russia: censorship, secret police, the entanglements of bureaucratic incompetence, an all-powerful and brutal autocracy. This book of mine assumes throughout that an important step in progress... had occurred, that nothing in our human history would ever be the same.

Now, with a changed mind, Wilson writes that the book is at least a basically reliable account of what reformers, revolutionary theorists and conspirators in Europe, and eventually in Russia, 'thought they were doing' in the nineteenth century in the interests of ' "a better world" '. His precise criticisms are that he undoubtedly underrated the vigorous persistence of the French Socialist tradition and sinned in leaving out Jaurès and Zola, and that his dislike of the Abbé Coignard and *Le Petit Pierre* made him underrate Anatole France of the *Histoire Contemporaine* and *Les Dieux Ont Soif*. I myself would have said that there is rather much of the gourmet in Anatole France's manner when he dwells on the sexual gratifications of massacre. A Goya saw terror as open nightmare: the fact that violence devours its children was neither a metaphor nor a psychological conceit to the Spaniard; in the indignation of Anatole France there is also a smell of tooled leather in the library. As for the charge that Wilson was too amiable to Lenin, Wilson admits that the critics have some grounds for saying this, but he had had, at the time, only the accounts authorized by the Soviet Government! With the truly Wilsonian appetite for new documents, he now adds several views of Lenin by people who knew him. He quotes a long passage from Pyotr Struve, a Russian contemporary, who said that in his attitude to his fellow-men Lenin 'breathed coldness, contempt, and cruelty'. This was bound up with his love of power. Another writer, recounting what he knew of the decision to kill the Czar and his family said:

In the intellectual circles of the Party there probably were misgivings and shakings of heads. But the masses of workers and soldiers had not a minute's doubt. They would not have understood and would not have accepted any other decision. *This* Lenin sensed well. The ability to think and feel for and with the masses was characteristic of him to the highest degree, especially at the great political turning points.

Wilson's attentions to his critics are proper in their way, but not so very relevant; after all, the book ends with Lenin's dramatic arrival in Leningrad—a story told with all Wilson's glinting exactness—and says almost nothing about the Revolution itself. The originality of *To the Finland Station* lies not in its direct narrative or in its factuality but in its study of the writing and acting of history. The task Wilson sets himself is to follow the devious yet constantly renewed threads in the texture of conspiracy. His people and their actions are born when their minds make their act of discovery. So Vico, the modest Italian scholar who finds his academic career blocked because of his humble origins and because he is thought to be a crank, is driven into the wilderness where he discovers the subversive idea that society is organic: 'I speak of this incontestable truth: the social world is certainly the work of men'. This is in 1725. Then there is a leap to 1824, when Michelet, the son of a poor printer persecuted by Napoleon, finds Vico's name in a translator's note and—in brisk Wilsonian phrase— 'immediately set out to learn Italian'. History is born, and here, with Michelet as master, Wilson has half his method and strikes his subject. Michelet said that he dashed off his *Introduction to Universal History* when he was fresh from 'the burning pavements' of Paris and the workers' riots before Charles X abdicated, in 1830, and in the fervent chapters on Michelet's life and work one can see how much of Wilson's method was extracted and adapted from the historian. One main difference between Michelet's method and the method of the ordinary historian, Wilson says, is this:

The ordinary historian knows what is going to happen in the course of his historical narrative because he knows what has really happened, but Michelet is able to put us back at upper stages of the stream of time, so that we grope with the people of the past themselves, share their heroic faiths, are dismayed by their unexpected catastrophes, feel, for all our knowledge of after-the-event, that we do *not* know precisely what is coming. Michelet responds with the sensitivity of a poet to every change of tempo, movement or scope and he develops

an infinitely varied technique to register different phases. . . .
To give us a final symbol for the monarchy, Michelet has only
to describe without comment the expense and the clumsy
complication of the great waterworks at Marly which make
the Versailles fountains play and which fill the air for miles
around with their agonized creakings and groanings.

Wilson was no poet; he was a humane critic, but how
closely his thinking method follows what in Michelet was
learnedly emotional.

So, in Wilson's powerful essay, Michelet the historian is
seen as a character playing a personal and creative part himself
in history. He is a human continuation of it. Very early on in
the book, we see him as both man and symbol. There he stands
for us—the laborious and fervid son of a printer worshipping
his father's printing press itself. It might be some allegorical
object out of Balzac. The press represents enlightenment and
liberty. When Napoleon's police took the whole family off to
jail and put the seals on the machine 'the incident caused Jules
such anguish that he afterwards made a stipulation in his will
that his wife should not be obliged to seal his coffin'. When
Wilson moves on to Renan, Taine, France and, briefly, to the
Symbolists in order to show the ossification of the once
Romantic impulse, the biographical detail links their thinking
to their lives. And biography plays a major part as his grand
examination of Babeuf, Marx, Engels, Bakunin, Lassalle,
Lenin and Trotsky expands. It is amusingly typical of Wilson
that he should turn to one of Meredith's novels for an oblique
glance at Lassalle.

Wilson was not, in the academic sense, a scholar or historian. He was an enormous reader, one of those readers who
are perpetually on the scent from book to book. He was the
old-style man of letters, but galvanized and with the iron of
purpose in him. He was proud of his journalistic alacrity and
of the gift of combining symphonic effects with those of 'no

comment'. One has read dozens of books about the development of Socialist thought; one's mind is a sort of photograph album of the riots, risings, and coups d'état: Wilson takes this for granted. He brings us something else: intimacy with the makers. He is a critic in whom history is broken up into minds. And despite the awkwardness of his prose, he is a coherent artist in the architecture of his subject. I mean that he is an artist—this is evident in so much of his writing—in the sense that he is a man possessed. Give him the subject and it fuses with his whole person as if something like Mesmer's famous magnetic fluid had flowed into him. The effect is all the stronger because he is not exalted; he is, indeed, phlegmatic, as if his whole idea were a matter of grasp. He is as penetrating and as summary as the lawyer or the doctor (there is a good deal of both in him): sceptical, pungent, even dry as he surveys the evidence. Then the artist blows and puts the glow of life into it and the critic sets the perspective. An egotist himself, he understands that the egotism of his conspirators is a passion and a fate.

This is what gives his long, argued portraits of Marx and Engels their supreme and moving place in the book. Here, in fact, are Michelet-like figures who do not know what will happen, and who had actually thought of Russia as a bugbear. Being Germans, Marx and Engels had a cultivated contempt for the Slavs. Marx had pinned his hopes on *Das Kapital*'s being published in English! It was not published in England in his lifetime yet from England he had drawn a huge part of his evidence, and when he heard of the Russian translation he complained that the Russians 'always run after the most extreme ideas that the West has to offer'. How tenderly, but without infatuation, Wilson follows the devotion of Engels to Marx's overwhelming labours. Marx felt that he was borne down by an incubus. Wilson's criticism is searching, but not destructive; it enlarges our sense of the intellectual and human drama of Marx's life; both his morbid personal hatreds *and* his idealizing of necessity are organically part of a passion. Even the boils, the carbuncles, the rheumatism, the enlarged liver, the markedly sadistic metaphors of his prose, his guilt—all are part of the struggle. Marx groaned that he was a non-God-fearing Job. There is a background of myth and even of mysticism in the elusive and supposedly scientific idea of the Dialectic, the mystery of the Trinity reborn. Wilson goes on to write:

> No: he is not so god-fearing. He sees himself also as 'Old Nick', the Goethean spirit that denies. Yet Old Nick is not the right symbol either: this Devil has been twisted and racked. . . . It is Prometheus who remains his favourite hero; for Prometheus is a Satan who suffers, a Job who never assents; and, unlike either Job or Satan, he brings liberation to mankind. Prometheus turns up in *Das Kapital* (in Chapter 23) to represent the proletariat chained to capital. The Light-Bringer was tortured, we remember, by Zeus's eagle's tearing, precisely, his liver, as Karl Marx himself—who is said to have reread Aeschylus every year—was obsessed by the fear that his liver would be eaten, like his father's, by cancer. And yet, if it is a devouring bird which Father Zeus has sent against the rebel, it is also a devourer, a destroyer, fire, which Prometheus has brought to man. And in the meantime the deliverer is never delivered; the slayer never rises from the grave. The resurrection, although certain, is not yet; for the expropriators are yet to be expropriated.

But before Wilson goes on to inquire into the failure of Marx's drastic dogma when it meets the resilience of advanced industrial societies, he reminds us that the importance of a book depends on the depths from which it is drawn:

> Only so sore and angry a spirit, so ill at ease in the world, could have recognized and seen into the causes of the wholesale mutilation of humanity, the grim collisions, the uncomprehended convulsions, to which that age of great profits was doomed.

Michelet, Wilson says, had tried to relive the past as an artistic creation, an attempt that was to make a strong impression on Proust—and had seen history break the pattern. Would Lenin be able to impose not an artistic pattern but one of political direction? Of all the Marxists, Lenin was the least in love with prophetic visions. ('Theoretical classification doesn't matter now'.) And there, artistically, Wilson's symphony comes to an end, not with a crescendo or a crash of cymbals but, rather, leaving us to move out of biography, impression, the books, the conspiracy, to the frightful territory where history, like nature, is red in tooth and claw. The Wilson of 1940 thought that we must not be surprised if later events were not to be 'amenable' to the pattern either of the vision or of practice. In 1971 Wilson, the battered liberal, *is* surprised at the appearance of 'one of the most hideous tyrannies that the world had ever known'.

To the Finland Station is perhaps the only book on the grand scale to come out of the Thirties—in either England or America. It contains to a novel degree the human history of an argument, from its roots to its innumerable branches, domestic and emotional. It comes from a mind that is divided between something like an obsession with record for its own sake and the drastic habit of imposing a personal emotion. Yet, in the writing, simply because of the profound instinct of an imagination that has lived in the sun of art and is unrepentant, fed by the intuitions and idiosyncrasies of the artist, the book is lifted, with a thinking excitement, from the ground. Again and again its sudden queer asides, its touches of vernacular pugnacity, its minuteness and—for that matter—its shrewdness, piety and goodwill mark it as deeply American. Even in style it is democratic, in the sense that this distinguished man will not for long allow one phrase to be better than another; the whole argument, as in narrative, must be plain-spoken and cogent. The histories of conspiracy have often attracted the rival angers of the orthodox and the fanatic or the dismissive wit of irony; none of these authors, in my recollection, emphasizes as Wilson does, that at the core of the history of the nineteenth century there is intellectual anguish, often ugly with the pain and vanity of human nature; if Europe was a brilliant assembly of courts and salons, with their commanding intellects, it was also—for the masses—half hospital, and in Russia almost all hospital. Wilson reminds us that Chekhov's *Ward No. 6* had a devastating effect on the mind of the young Lenin. It is because it never loses sight of the pain gnawing at the heart of the human conscience that Wilson's discursive record, untouched by rhetoric, achieves pages one can only call noble.

SAUL BELLOW

Jumbos

SAUL BELLOW HAS the most effusive intelligence of living
American novelists. Even when he is only clever he has a kind
of spirited intellectual vanity that enables him to take on all
the facts and theories about the pathetic and comically
exposed condition of civilized man and distribute them like
high-class corn so that the chickens come running to them.
That is the art of the novelist who can't resist an idea: to evoke,
attract that 'pleasing, anxious being', the squawking, dusty,
feverish human chicken. Aldous Huxley could always throw
the corn but nothing alive came fluttering to it.

But immensely clever novelists have to beware of self-
dispersal when they run to great length. I enjoy Saul Bellow in
his spreading carnivals and wonder at his energy, but I still
think he is finer in his shorter works. *The Victim* was the best
novel to come out of America—or England—for a decade.
The Dangling Man is good, but subdued; *Seize the Day* is a
small grey masterpiece. If one cuts out the end, *Henderson the
Rain King* is at once profound and richly diverting in its
fantasy. These novels had form; their economy drove their
point home. By brevity Bellow enhanced our experience.
And, to a European reader—though this may be irrelevant—he
seems the only American of this generation to convey the feel
and detail of urban America, preserving especially what is
going on at the times when nothing is going on: the distinctive native ennui, which is the basic nutriment of any national
life.

It is when he turns to longer books, chasing the mirage of
'the great American novel', that Bellow weakens as he becomes

a traveller, spreading the news and depending on the presence of a character who is something like a human hold-all, less a recognizable individual than a fantastic piece of bursting luggage. His labels, where he has been, whom he has met in his collision with America are more suggestive than his banal personal story. In *Herzog*, the hero or rather the grandiose victim, is a gifted Jewish professor and polymath with a rather solemn pretension to sexual prowess. He seems a promising exemplar of the human being exposed to everything without the support of a settled society or fixed points of belief or value. This theme has offered the American novelist a chance to show his vitality for a long time now and the Jewish novelists have done strikingly well with it, for as a group they have acutely felt the sense of a missing law or covenant.

What has happened to Moses Herzog, this restless dabbler in the ideas of four centuries? He is having a breakdown because his second wife has destroyed his sexual confidence. He sees himself—and Mr Bellow sees him—prancing through one marriage and several liaisons with success and then marrying the all-time bitch; exhibitionist, hysteric, looter of his brain, spender of his money, far-seeing in matters of law and property, adulterous, glamorously second-rate but adroit with the castrating scissors. To add insult, not to mention symbolism, to injury, the man she goes off with is a one-legged radio phoney. The ruthless and learned Moses, a walking university, begins to look like a Jumboburger who has been told he has lost his mustard. His earlier women may say 'Serve him right', but neither they nor the reader are likely to think his sufferings of much importance when, in a ham ending, he solemnly shacks up with a tremendously international woman called Ramona—of all names—who is apt to come swaggering out of the bathroom with her hand on her hip like a dagger-carrying flamenco dancer, and wearing black frilly panties with saucy ribbons. Twice during the novel she clinches the entire deal by serving the gourmet the only dish, apparently, she knows how to cook: Shrimp Arnaud, washed down with a bottle of Pouilly Fuissé. His earlier ladies must have thought they had paid a high price. Why didn't they think of applying this particular nostrum to the exposed soul of modern man? One knows that the fantasy life of university professors is often surprisingly gaudy, that the minds of experts on seventeenth-century thought or the *condition humaine* often drift off to Hollywood in the evenings. If this is Mr Bellow's ironical realism it certainly describes the feeble state of contemporary erotic fancy: but I detect no irony. Yet irony and self-irony are usually Mr Bellow's strength. What is more, the one or two love affairs in the book suggest that Moses is looking for easily punishable women without his or Mr Bellow's knowing it. In a moment of insight Moses wonders if his obsession with sex and love isn't really feminine. The reader is likely to go further and ask whether Moses is not hermaphrodite.

Structurally and in content, the story of *Herzog* is unsustaining. But what Herzog sees, the accidental detail of his experience, is very impressive. Here he grows. He really has got a mind and it is hurt. It is a tribute to Mr Bellow's reserves of talent that the novel survives and over-grows its own weaknesses. The muddle Moses is in, his sense of victimization, are valuable. His paranoia is put, by Mr Bellow, to excellent use. If the theme is lost, we have the American scene. Moses is not really exposed, but his New York and Chicago are. Mr Bellow has something like a genius for place. There is not a descriptive insinuator of what, say, a city like New York is like from minute to minute who comes anywhere near him. Some novelists stage it, others document it; he is breathing in it. He knows how to show us not only Moses but other people, moving from street to street, from room to room in their own circle of uncomprehending solitude. Grasping this essential of life in a big city he sees the place not as a confronted

whole, but continually askance. His senses are especially alive
to *things* and he catches the sensation that the *things* have
created the people or permeated them. This was the achievement of *The Victim*, and it is repeated in *Herzog*. A wanderer,
he succeeds with minor characters, the many small figures in
the crowd who suggest millions more. The dialogue of a
Puerto Rican taxi driver, a Chicago cop, a low lawyer, a
Jewish family, people brash, shady or saddened by the need of
survival and whose ripeness comes out of the dirty brick that
has trapped them, is really wonderful. It is far superior to
Hemingway's stylized naturalism: Bellow's talk carries the
speaker's life along with it. Their talk makes them move.
They involve Moses with themselves and show him living, as
all human beings do, in a web spun by others as well as by
himself.

The habit of seeing things askance or out of the corner of his
eye has given Mr Bellow an even more important quality: it
keeps alive a perpetual sense of comedy and feeds his
originality. There is sometimes talk of a taste for elegance in
his book; spoken of like that, as a sort of craving or innate
possession, it sounds very nearly vulgar. But there is an
implicit elegance of mind in his writing: it sharpens the comic
edge and dares him to spirited invention. As far as the comedy
is concerned it has all the fatality of Jewish comedy, that
special comedy of human undress and nakedness of which the
Jewish writers are the world's masters. The other gift of Mr
Bellow is his power of fantastic invention. He has hit upon a
wonderful device for conveying Herzog's nervous breakdown.
How to deal with his paranoia—if that is what it is—how to
make it contribute not only to the character of Herzog but
also to the purpose of the book? Mr Bellow decides that
Herzog's dottiness shall consist in writing unfinished letters
to all kinds of people living and dead, known and unknown—
to his women friends, to editors, tutors, professors, philosophers, to his dead mother, to the President. It is the habit of

the mad and Moses is not mad; but he at once is comically and seriously disturbed by every kind of question. Is romanticism 'spilt religion'? 'Do the visions of genius become the canned goods of intellectuals?' He writes to Eisenhower asking him 'to make it all clear in a few words'. He begins addressing M. de Jouvenal about the aims of political philosophy. The letters are really the scribbles of an exhausted mind. Travelling in the subway Moses evokes the dream figure of a Dr Shrödinger at Times Square:

> It has been suggested [and why not] that reluctance to cause pain is actually an extreme form, a delicious form of sensuality, and that we increase the luxuries of pain by the injection of a moral pathos. Thus working both sides of the street. Nevertheless, there are moral realities, Herzog assured the entire world as he held his strap in the speeding car.

Since Moses is a man of intellect these addresses are often interesting in themselves; but chiefly they convey the dejected larking of a mind that has been tried by two contradictory forces: the breakdown of the public world we live in and the mess of private life. In which world does he live? He is absurd yet he is fine; he is conceited yet he is raw. He is a great man yet he is torpedoed by a woman who 'wants to live in the delirious professions'—trades in which the main instrument is your opinion of yourself and the raw material is your reputation or standing. At times he lives like a sort of high-class Leopold Bloom, the eternal Jewish clown; at others he is a Teufelsdröckh; again he is the pushing son of the bewildered Polish-Jewish immigrant and failed boot-legger, guilty about his break with the past, nagged by his relations, his ambitions punctured.

As a character Moses is physically exact—we know his domestic habits—but mentally and emotionally amorphous. Any objection to this is cancelled by his range as an observer-victim. It is a triumph that he is not a bore and does not ask our sympathy.

★   ★   ★

The outsize heroes of Bellow's long novels are essentially moral types who have been forced by the American scene to behave like clowns. They are the classic American monologue in person, elephantine chunks of ego. In *Humboldt's Gift* we meet the clown as performing poet:

> A wonderful talker, a hectic non-stop monologist and improvisator, a champion detractor: to be loused up by Humboldt was really a kind of privilege. It was like being the subject of a two-nosed portrait by Picasso or an eviscerated chicken by Soutine. . . .

One recognizes the voice at once: it has the dash, the dandyism, the easy control of side-slipping metaphor and culture-freaking which gives pace to Saul Bellow's comedies. He is above all a performer, and in *Humboldt's Gift* he tells the story of performance in the person of Citrine, Humboldt's worshipper, disciple and betrayer.

As a youth Citrine had kneeled before the great manic depressive who had passed the peak of his reputation and was left, gin bottle in hand, cursing American materialism for what it does to genius and the life of the imagination. Humboldt was shrewd enough to see that the young Citrine was on the make, but was glad to have an ally among the young: everything went well, in a general alcoholic way, until Citrine did a frightful thing: he wrote a Broadway success which made him a sudden fortune. He had gone straight to the top of the tree. This was more than the crumbling, middle-aged poet could bear: he did not mind that Citrine had portrayed him as a knockabout Bohemian character; what he resented was the money going into Citrine's pocket. By this time Humboldt has become the classic American drunken genius and hospital case who shows up American philistinism. Getting out of Bellevue, Humboldt has a delightful time with the psychiatrists:

> Even the shrewd Humboldt knew what he was worth in professional New York. Endless conveyor belts of sickness or litigation poured clients and patients into these midtown offices like dreary Long Island potatoes. These dull spuds crushed psychoanalysts' hearts with boring character problems. Then suddenly Humboldt arrived. Oh Humboldt! He was no potato! He was papaya, a citron, a passion fruit. . . . And what a repertory he had, what changes of style and tempo. He was meek at first—shy. Then he became child-like, trusting, then he confided. . . . He said he knew what husbands and wives said when they quarrelled. . . . People said ho-hum and looked at the ceiling when you started this. Americans! With their stupid ideas about love and their domestic tragedies. How could you bear to listen to them after the worst of wars and the most sweeping of revolutions, the destruction, the death camps, the earth soaked in blood. . . . The world looked into American faces and said: 'Don't tell me these cheerful, well-to-do people are suffering. . . . Anyway I'm not here to discuss adolescent American love-myths'—this was how Humboldt talked. Still, he said, I'd like you to listen to this.

And, suddenly blazing up, he howled out all the melodramas of American scandal and lust. The lawyers had heard it a thousand times—but they wanted to hear it again from a man of genius. He had become what the respectable professionals long for—their pornographer.

As admirers of Saul Bellow's work know, he is a master of elaborately patterned narrative that slips back or forward in time, circulating like Sterne, like Proust even. Sterne did this because he loved human inertia: Bellow is out for every tremor of the over-electrified American ego: he is expert in making characters disappear and then reappear swollen and with palms itching for more and more instant life. Humboldt will die in an elevator, but he will haunt the novel to the end like Moby Dick: even contemporary ghosts are jumbo size. The story moves to Chicago and there, on native ground, Citrine fills out. He is Cleverness and Success in person:

> It was my turn to be famous and to make money, to get heavy mail, to be recognised by influential people, to be dined at Sardis and propositioned in padded booths by women who sprayed themselves with musk, to buy Sea Island cotton underpants and leather luggage.

His troubles with the tax man, with his ex-wife's lawyers who are stripping him of everything they can get hold of, seem to excite rather than depress him. His sexual life is avid and panicky: he hopes to outsmart middle age. He has bouts of hypochondria. These are enjoyable because he is very frank about his vanity: his touchiness, as middle age comes on, is the making of him as a comic figure. Gleam as he may with success, he cherishes what his wife calls his 'cemetery bit'; he has a bent for being a victim: ironical and sentimental, he also knows he is as hardheaded as that other famous twelve-year-old charmer, David Copperfield.

Once Humboldt is dead, Citrine is without a necessary enemy, and here Mr Bellow makes a very interesting find: Rinaldo Cantabile, a small crook with the naïve notion that he can 'make' the top Mafia. Unlike Humboldt, there is nothing myth-attracting in Cantabile. He is a loud, smart, nasty smell; he understands the first lesson of gangsterdom: to humiliate your victim; but he is an ass. We remember that Citrine is out to explore the American love–hate of Culture and Genius and indeed takes us round colleges and foundations: Cantabile is introduced to suggest that the Mafia might get a foot in here. Cantabile even thinks he can terrorize Citrine into seeing that Cantabile's wife gets a Ph.D by fraud. My own view is that he does not make the grade as a compelling menace: he is without the extra dimension given to Bellow's strongly felt characters.

However, good comes of Cantabile, for he gets Mr Bellow back to Chicago. That city is the hero of *Humboldt's Gift*. No American novelist surpasses Bellow in the urban scene. He knows Chicago intimately from the smell of old blood in the hot nights from the rust on its fire escapes and the aluminium glint of the Lake. He knows the saunas:

> the wooden posts were slowly consumed by a wonderful decay that made them soft brown. They looked like beavers' fur in the golden vapour. . . . The Division-Street steam-bathers don't look like the trim proud people downtown. . . . They are vast in antique form. They stand on thick pillow legs affected with a sort of creeping verdigris or blue-cheese mottling of the ankles . . . you feel these people are almost conscious of obsolescence, of a time of civilisation abandoned by nature and culture. So down in the super-heated sub cellars all these Slavonic cavemen and wood demons with hanging laps of fat and legs of stone and lichen, boil themselves and splash ice-water on their heads by the bucket. Upstairs, on the television screen in the locker room, dudes and grinning broads make smart talk or leap up and down. . . . Below, Franush, the attendant, makes steam by sloshing water on the white-hot boulders.

The secret of Mr Bellow's success is that he talks people into life and never stops pouring them in and out of his scenes. In this book the women are particularly well-drawn. Citrine's sexual vanity is a help here: once satisfied, he is taken aback by the discovery that women have other interests—the delightful delinquent Demmie is reformed, but in sleep at night her buried life comes out in groans and howls as she wrestles with the devil, and she wakes up next day fresh as a daisy to get down on her knees for redemption by scrubbing floors. Denise is the climbing wife of the climbing man. Vassar girl, seductive and respectable—what more does she want? The ear of top people at the White House: she wants to tell them what she has just read in *Newsweek*! And then Renata—a fate for more than one Bellow hero—Spanishy, flamenco-ish, vulgar, genial, sexually voracious, knows her Ritzes, and while willing to listen to high-class intellectual talk for a while, makes it clear that her price is very high and her fidelity at perpetual risk. These women are real, even likeable. Why? I think because in some clever way Mr Bellow shows them moving through their own peculiar American day, which is unlike the day of Citrine. One might press the point further and say that Bellow's characters are real to us because they are physical objects—Things. What other tenderness can a materialist society contain?

It says a great deal for Bellow's gift that although he can raise very boring subjects and drop names like an encyclo-paedia or a digest, he has tact and irony. He is crisp. But two-thirds of the way through this novel he lands himself with a tangle of dramatic situations as complex as, say, the last act of a Restoration comedy. Here he lost me. Humboldt—it turns out—had repented of calling Citrine a Judas and traitor; had even left him a money-making film script—put into the hands of the right phoney director it should make a fortune. It does. Citrine does not take the money, indeed he behaves so well that it looks as though in saving his soul from corruption he may lose Renata. One curious act he does perform: he has Humboldt and his mother disinterred and re-buried in a decent cemetery. That's one thing you can do for artists.

MARY McCARTHY

A Quiet American

THE TITLE OF Mary McCarthy's *Birds of America* makes clear
that this is an ironical ornithology of certain American species
on their contemporary feeding grounds in New England,
Paris and Rome. It is really an 'education sentimentale' of a
young American bird watcher, Peter Levi. He is literally that.
From boyhood his lonely, seeking mind is haunted by the
lusts of the Great Horned Owl, the ancient knowledge of the
cormorant. His talented twice-divorced mother, who is 'perfect' in her divorce—no alimony—and who is 'too good to be
true' is, for him, a rose-breasted grosbeak; the hard-drinking
local Admiral with his horrible curries and his telescope has
'the hoarse voice of a sea bird'. Not for nothing is the
cormorant dying out. Not for nothing at the end of the book
has young Peter Levi, lying in a fever at a Paris hospital, been
injured by an angry swan in the Jardin des Plantes. Not for
nothing in his delirium does he see his favourite philosopher,
Kant, crawling up the coverlet with the news that God is
dead—everyone knows that—but that Nature is dead too.

As a bird himself Peter belongs to the tame young
American Candide group. Well-educated by elusive academic
parents, intelligent, driven by conscience and maxims—Treat
no one as a Means: Not to Care is a Sin—without vanity or
conceit trying to make up a virginal mind, Peter has, for the
moment, the neutered air of his type. He has a much better
brain than Candide had but he suffers from the fact that his
bustling elders have gobbled up the store of family passion
and vitality for the moment. All their passions have left him
with is Reason.

Rosamund, his mother, the grosbeak, has had two Jewish husbands, the second a German physicist. She has separated from them—one never hears what went on—and is seen early on scrupulously trying not to be married to her son. She will find a third partner and become a famous international harpsichord player. An old American story: the boy is left serious but happy in his loneliness, for personal relations have been disinfected. By the time he is nineteen the youth has an elderly view of his mother. 'Her faults pleased him' but

... he had become cautious about her, not trusting her sweetness and unruffled temper. Besides her faults were no longer familiar. He recognised them in himself. Her zeal to please had set him a bad example. It made him placatory. Her scruples in him had become irresolution and an endless picking at himself like masturbation—a habit he had not completely outgrown and which seemed to him ignominious, even though she and the *babbo* [his father, the Italian Jew] had said it was natural in puberty; on that score he felt they had given him a wrong steer. Moreover her good qualities [she was generous to a fault] did not inspire imitation. Rather the contrary.... He admired his father for having the strength of his defects.

Peter 'really loved his mother for having the faults of America', summed up in the word 'extravagance'. Puritanism was an extravagance, like Prohibition. Americans, the Babbo said, were logicians with no idea of limit.

So there at Rocky Port, Peter stands 'quarantined in history' in a fading New England where his mother is beautifully stirring up trouble because the old foods and recipes are giving place to awful packaged mixes. The old New England is being replaced by the commercially historic for the summer residents. Tradition itself has become a product.

The word *tradition* was often heard at Rocky Port cocktail parties, usually on the lips of a woman with blue hair or a fat man in Polynesian shorts. The village was protecting its traditions, Peter was repeatedly told, as though Rocky Port were a sanctuary of banded birds, threatened with extirpation. He wondered what had been handed down to these people and what they were safeguarding—except money. There was nothing distinctive about Rocky Port's way of life, unless it was the frequency of gift shops for selling 'gourmet' foods, outsize pepper mills, 'amusing aprons' and chefs' costumes, bar equipment and frozen croissants 'just like in France' . . . Rocky Port was a museum.

All this is Miss McCarthy with the claws just showing and it is very funny but what will happen to the innocent Peter when he gets abroad? He is wide open to disaster and, in a vulgar way, we hope for it. He is rather English Public Schoolboy, Huxley type, *circa* 1925. He will have small misadventures, like failing to realize his dream of crossing France on his motor bike and other comedies of youthful shyness, but Miss McCarthy is out for his education. The book is partly a *Bildungsroman* of the young man who meets the wrong people abroad and who will discover that the modern world is polluted by unsolved questions. Human beings themselves are becoming a kind of mass garbage.

We settle down to one of Miss McCarthy's sharp-eyed commentaries of travel. Peter asks questions about equality, education, politics, mass society, and so on, and since he is a touching, fidgeting and exceptional young man, he finds more and more to worry about. We are on his side all the time. When goaded he can burst out at an awful Thanksgiving dinner in Paris—one of the high satirical moments of the book —and he is a wicked listener. (Getting information embarrasses him because it feels like espionage: this is one of Miss McCarthy's excellent insights into a thoughtful young man's mind and indeed, throughout, in preserving its elderliness, she has really brought out the half-resentful charm of youth.) Although it can be said that his scruples insure him against any danger of chancing his arm, Peter is an extremist in his own way. He has inherited the national obsession with plumbing from his mother and, in Paris hotels, has a comic and philosophical bout of compulsive toilet cleaning. He is certainly not earthy about 'night soil'; but he does wonder whether his cleaning up after others isn't undemocratic, i.e. being cleaner than others. If he is a prig he is an original. There is his care for a Fatsheara, a plant, a species of ivy which he tries to keep alive in his dark room. It begins to get leggy. The scene that follows might come out of that delightful Victorian conversation piece, *Sandford and Merton*:

> The leaves at the base were falling off one by one, and though he had been carefully irritating the stem at the base to produce a new sideward growth, it had been ignoring this prodding on his part and just getting taller, weed-like, till he finally had the idea of taking it for walks, once or twice a week, depending on the weather. . . . He thought he was beginning to note signs of gratitude in the invalid for the trouble he was taking . . . there was a detectable return of chlorophyll, like a green flush to the cheeks of the shut-ins. He spoke to it persuasively—sometimes out loud—urging it to grow. So far, he had resisted giving it a shot of fertiliser, because a mildewed American manual he had acquired on the *quais*—How to Care For Your House Plants—cautioned against giving fertiliser except to 'healthy subjects'. That would be like giving a gourmet dinner to a starving person—the old parable of the talents.

This plant-walking saves him when he runs into a student riot. The thing has grown tall and guarantees his innocence to the bored *flics*. Naturally he has already got in touch with French bird watchers, most respectably, through the Embassy. How odd that regard for embassies strikes a European! Practical, of course.

But the American bird abroad tends to the flaunting species of the turkey. Peter soon runs into it gobbling in its European farmyard. He goes to an awful Thanksgiving dinner given, without the art that conceals art, by a General who would like to swap the war in Vietnam for the real thing. Here the narrative breaks into broad farce. The General's son—a problem boy who has failed college, can't get a job: he simply collects parking tickets—has volunteered for Vietnam. His mother drinks his health:

'It was Benjy's own decision. "I've got to go, Mom," he said. Leonard wanted us to refuse our consent though he's only Benjy's stepfather. "Let him wait till he's drafted," Leonard said. But I couldn't say "No" to Benjy. . . . I guess I've spoiled him: he's my only child.' Her face which might have been pretty when she was young, crinkled and puckered like a wide seersucker bedspread.

Benjy is guzzling pie and ice cream: his 'wine-intake had been monitored by his mother'.

It came as a surprise to Peter that contrary to what you would expect in such a milieu, Benjy's parents were far from being proud of the patriot they had fledged. Even if he came back covered with medals he would not get the fatted calf. To hear his mother tell it, she spent most of her time on her knees praying for peace. 'Though Benjy doesn't like me to do it. He hates it if I go into some little church and light a candle.' 'Yeah, I want to get some of those gorillas fast'. 'Guerrillas, please, Benjy.' She gave the 'l's' a Spanish pronunciation. 'He used to think they were real gorillas,' she explained with a little gurgle of a laugh. 'He got it from listening to the radio.'

In the same scene there is a vegetarian girl, a heretic at the national feast; Peter rather falls for her and 'has a new worry: as an animal lover how can he justify eating meat?' We also get a glimpse of private life in NATO. Peter's neighbour at the dinner is a leathery lady whose husband has gone off with a German.

'He wants a divorce, but if I give him a divorce, they'll take away my PX card and my Q.C. privileges. You can smile, Peter, but to me it's a tragedy.... Civilians don't dig what it means to us. Chuck and Letitia can entertain lavishly because, unlike you and me, they don't buy a thing on the French market. Not even a stick of celery.'

Ordinarily Peter would have felt sorry for this coarse-grained Donna Elvira. Maybe she loved the guy and was ashamed to mention that: it was odd what people were ashamed of, sometimes the best part of themselves.

The Sorbonne, so far as Peter's fellow Americans are concerned, is a shambles. The University cynically takes the fees, knowing the students will do nothing, but will kid themselves that they are absorbing something or other unconsciously. Peter can't make up his mind about this. In Rome, which he enjoys more than Paris, he meets a real stinker in the mean figure of Mr Small. Mr Small hangs about the galleries and cafés, insinuating himself among the young and getting information about student life and needs. At the right point, he takes down what they say on tape.

He quickly decides Peter is so abnormal that he needs a psychiatrist, but Peter is now in good condition for an argument. He discovers Mr Small is doing research for a Foundation which has a tie-up with hotels, travel agencies, advertisers and airlines. The motive? To follow and quietly direct the migration routes of these young birds and to capture and exploit the student traffic. Mass student transport under the direction of mass society, the old Conference trick!

The dreadful question of tourism arises. The Sistine Chapel is full of garbage—human garbage. An art lover cannot see the pictures. People are polluting the planet, because it pays to pollute it. Peter thinks enviously of Milton who was said to have travelled with a hermit. Doesn't Mr Small occasionally get scared, asks Peter, the protector of the human bird sanctuary. Mr Small replies:

'Scared? I can't think of a more challenging time to be alive for an American. All the options are open. No society in history before our own has given so-called mass man such opportunities for self realisation.' 'To me everything is closing in,' Peter argued. 'If I were a Russian or a Pole at least I might have the illusion that things would be better if there was a revolution. Or even gradual evolution. But here evolution just means more of the same. . . .'

Peter does adroitly prevent Mr Small from putting down his lunch to Mr Small's expense account. The scrupulous have to rely on a small victory here and there.

One is waiting for Peter to commit at least one rash act. Love has escaped him. While he wavered, his vegetarian girl has gone off with a Frenchman and one half-expects the boy to rescue a fallen woman. He does—but she is no more than a reeking female *clochard* whom he allows to spend a night on the floor of his room. She rewards his charity by stealing his door knob, a clever move in a small-minded way. (Strange that it should puzzle him.)

So we leave this quiet American to be rescued by his immensely successful mother and the dream figure of Kant. He points out to her irritably that he was not *bitten* by a swan; swans strike, they do not bite. (Not, I believe, true; I was bitten by one when I was eight.) He will return home from studying the American bird abroad to face college and the Army.

Miss McCarthy has really rediscovered an old form of travel commentary in giving Peter her own critical detachment and knowledge; but it doesn't matter that Peter is too precocious and, like his mother, too good to be true. He is a relief after the showy, self-dramatizing confessionals and sexual loud-mouths. A late developer, he enjoys and profits by the virginity that his learned and irresponsible, rational parents have unwittingly loaded him with. If he is a tame bird, he is very touching in his dignity. He is too absorbed by what he sees to be self-pitying. Goodness knows how he has missed the morbidity of youth—perhaps that is a loss for him and even a mistake on Miss McCarthy's part, but one is glad to be spared it. He is just the shy young pedant to keep a topical allegory about intellectual pollution from being a bore. In a novel he would be thin, as he is; but in the Euro-American laboratory he is a ready piece of Puritan litmus.

FLANNERY O'CONNOR

Satan Comes to Georgia

ON THE WHOLE, English writers were slow starters in the art of the short story. Until Stevenson, Kipling and then D. H. Lawrence appeared, our taste was for the ruminative and disquisitional; we preferred to graze on the large acreage of the novel and even tales by Dickens or Thackeray or Mrs Gaskell strike us as being unused chapters of longer works. Free of our self-satisfactions in the nineteenth century, American writers turned earlier to a briefer art which learned from transience, sometimes raw and journalistic but essentially poetic in the sense of being an instant response to the exposed human being. Where we were living in the most heavily wind-and-water-proofed society in the world, the American stood at the empty street corner on his own in a world which, compared with ours, was anarchic; and it was the opinion of Frank O'Connor, the Irish master, that anarchic societies are the most propitious for an art so fundamentally drawn to startling dramatic insights and the inner riot that may possess the lonely man or woman at some unwary moment in the hours of their day.

All the characters in the very powerful stories of Flannery O'Connor—*Everything That Rises Must Converge*—are exposed: that is to say they are plain human beings in whose fractured lives the writer has discovered an uncouth relationship with the lasting myths and the violent passions of human life. The people are rooted in their scene, but as weeds are rooted. It would be fashionable to call her stories Gothic: they certainly have the curious inner strain of fable—replacing the social interest which is a distinguishing quality of the American

novel. (She herself was an invalid most of her life and died in
her native Georgia in 1964 at the age of 38.) The Southern
writers have sometimes tended to pure freakishness or have
concentrated on the eccentricities of a decaying social life: but
this rotting and tragic order has thrown up strong, if
theatrical, themes. Flannery O'Connor was born too late to be
affected by the romantic and nostalgic legend of the tragic
South: the grotesque for its own sake means nothing to her.
It is a norm. In the story called *Parker's Back*, an ignorant
truck-driver has indulged a life-long mania for getting tattooed
and in a desperate attempt to reawaken the interest of his pious
wife who had once been captivated, as other women had been,
by this walking art gallery, he has one final huge tattoo done
on his naked back which up till then had been a blank wall.
He pays for the most expensive tattoo there is: a Byzantine
Christ. She throws him out because he has revealed himself as
an idolater. The point of this story is not that it is bizarre: the
point is that, perhaps because of the confused symbols that
haunt the minds of the Bible Belt people, an inarticulate man
can wish to convey to her that, as a graven image, he is
indifferent to God and the Day of Judgment. He has some
claim to an inner life of his own. He wishes to show that he is
someone. He has burst the limits imposed on him. The act is
an agonized primitive appeal. It is also a childish act of
defiance and hatred.

The passions are just beneath the stagnant surface in
Flannery O'Connor's stories. She was an old Catholic, not a
convert, in the South of the poor white of the Bible Belt and
this gave her a critical skirmishing power. But the symbolism
of religion, rather than the acrimonies of sectarian dispute, fed
her violent imagination—the violence is itself oddly early
Protestant—as if she had seen embers of the burning Bible-fed
imagery in the minds of her own characters. The symbols are
always ominous: at sunset a wood may be idyllic, but also look
blood-sodden. They usually precede an act of violence which

will introduce the character at the end of the story 'into the world of guilt and sorrow'. This is her ground as a fabulist or moralist. We are left with an illusion shattered, with the chilly task of facing our hatreds. In one story, a priest comes to visit an unbeliever who is fanatically keen to die in order to punish his mother for having emasculated him. The man is cured by the local doctor whom he despises. We leave him on his death-bed but not dying:

> He saw that for the rest of his days, frail, racked, but enduring, he would live in the face of a purifying terror. A feeble cry, a last impossible protest escaped him. But the Holy Ghost emblazoned in ice instead of fire, continued implacably, to descend.

The essence of Flannery O'Connor's vision is that she sees terror as a purification—unwanted, of course: it is never the sado-masochist's intended indulgence. The moment of purification may actually destroy; it will certainly show someone changed.

Symbolism has been fatal to many writers: it offers a quick return of unearned meaning. I am not convinced by the theatrical entrance of the Holy Ghost in the above quotation. But elsewhere, whenever one detects a symbol, one is impressed by Flannery O'Connor's use of it: it is concrete and native to the text. Take the title story of the book: a middle-aged widow, dressed up in an awful new hat, is seen going with her son to a slimming class in order to get her high blood pressure down. She is a 'Southern lady' in reduced circumstances and now, bitterly but helplessly opposed to Negro integration, she sticks to her dignity. 'If you know who you are, you can go anywhere. . . . I can be gracious to anybody. I know who I am.' This is true, in a way, but it is also a cliché, as her son tells her while they travel on the integrated local bus. Here a disturbing figure appears: a Negro woman with her child.

She had on a hideous hat. A purple flap came down on one side of it and stood up on the other; the rest of it was green like a cushion with the stuffing out.

The hat is exactly a replica of the white woman's hat. To her son this is comical; it ought to teach his silly mother a lesson in racialism. The Negro woman's child sees the joke too. The white woman becomes gracious to the child and prepares to do a terrible, gracious thing: to give the little child a bright new penny. When they all get off the bus she does this. The huge Negro woman, seeming 'to explode like a piece of machinery that had been given one ounce of pressure too much', knocks the white woman down. Her son, who has hated his mother for years, sees a reality kill his mother and his own guilt.

Many of the stories are variations on the theme of the widowed mother who has emasculated her son; or the widower who is tragically unaware of what he is doing to his child. In one instance, a widower destroys his grandchild. These stories are not arguments; they are not case-histories or indignation meetings. They are selected for the claustrophobic violence which will purify but destroy. The characters are engaged in a struggle for personal power which they usually misunderstand. A mature and sensible young historian living with his mother is maddened by her naïve and reckless do-gooding behaviour. She rescues an amoral girl who calls herself a 'nimpermaniac' and has her to stay. The girl instantly makes a set at the historian who shows her that he hates her. There is a revolver in the house. Who will be killed? A probation officer—a widower—in another rescue story, takes into his house a young boy crook who introduces his son to fatal Bible Belt fantasies about Heaven and Hell—again, who will be killed? This story, particularly, is an attack on practical ethics as a substitute for religion: in another Art is shown to be inadequate as a substitute.

If these stories are anti-humanist propaganda one does not

notice it until afterwards. Like all Gothic writers, Flannery O'Connor has a deep sense of the Devil or rather of the multiplicity of devils, though not in any conventional religious sense. To the poor-white Gospellers, Satan has become Literature. For her the devils are forces which appear in living shape: the stray bull which kills the old farming widow whose sons let her down; the criminal child who is proud of being an irredeemable destroyer because he has been called a child of Satan, and looks forward, eagerly—it is his right—to an eternity in the flames of hell which he takes to be literal fire; the delinquent girl who has been taught by psychiatrists to regard her vice as an illness sees this as an emancipating distinction. The author is not playing the easy game of paradox which is commonly a tiresome element in the novels of Catholic converts: for her, the role of the diabolic is to destroy pride in a misconceived virtue.

A short story ought to be faultless without being mechanical. The wrong word, a misplaced paragraph, an inadequate phrase or a convenient explanation, start fatal leaks in this kind of writing which is formally very close to poetry. That closeness must be totally sustained. There are no faults of craftsmanship in Flannery O'Connor's stories. She writes a plain style: she has a remarkable ear for the talk of the poor whites, for the received ideas of the educated; and she creates emotion and the essence of people by vivid images. We see all the threatening sullen life of a poor farmer in this sentence: 'His plate was full but his fists sat motionless like two dark quartz stones on either side of it.' Since a short story must plant its situation—and promise another—in its opening lines, the passage at the beginning of *The Comforts of Home* is a model:

Thomas withdrew to the side of the window and with his head between the wall and the curtain he looked down on the driveway where the car had stopped. His mother and the little slut were getting out of it. His mother emerged slowly, stolid and awkward, and then the little slut's slightly bowed legs slid out, the dress pulled above the knees. With a shriek of laughter she ran to meet the dog who bounded, overjoyed, shaking with pleasure, to welcome her. Rage gathered throughout Thomas's large frame with a silent ominous intensity, like a mob assembling.

Thomas, an educated man, will find in fact that he has a mob buried in his unconscious. Flannery O'Connor is at pains to make us know intimately the lives of these poor white and struggling small-town people. They are there as they live, not in the interest of their ignorant normality, but in the interest of their exposure to forces in themselves that they do not yet understand. Satan, they will discover, is not just a word. He has legs—and those legs are their own.

SAMUEL PEPYS

The Great Snail

IT IS OBVIOUS from the three opening volumes that the new
complete eleven-volume edition of Pepy's Diary is an excellent
effort of Anglo-American scholarship. The omissions in earlier
editions, whether from prudery, accident or fear of tedium,
have been put back. The great difficulties of transcribing
Pepys's shorthand with its curious half-words 'in clear' have
been mastered as far as they can be; the innumerable notes are
irresistible, and Robert Latham's introduction of 120 pages is
by far the most searching and graceful essay available on the
diary in relation to Pepys himself and to history. It is particularly valuable on Pepys's methods. In short, full justice is
done to the Great Snail of English diarizing.

The only serious rival to Pepys is Boswell, but Boswell is a
snail without a shell. He trails through life unhoused and
exclamatory, whereas Pepys is housed and *sotto voce*. Boswell
is confessional before anything else, whereas, though he too
tells all, Pepys is not; he records for the sensual pleasure of
record. Boswell adores his damned soul to the point of tears
and is in shameless, ramshackle pursuit of father-figures who
will offer salvation. Unlike Pepys, he has above all a conceit
of his own peculiar genius. Pepys has no notion of genius.
Where Pepys is an eager careerist, struck by the wonder of it,
Boswell has no career; he has only a carousel, and it is odd that
the careerist has a more genuine sense of pleasure than the
Calvinist libertine. Although both diarists are lapsed Puritans
and owe something to the Puritan tradition of the diary as a
training of conscience, Pepys writes without appealing to
some private higher hope. He is as obsessional as Boswell,

but to whom is the secretive Admiralty official talking as his shorthand flicks across the page? To no person, not even to himself, even when he adds a remorseful groan or two, after running his hand up the skirt of a servant girl or the wife of an officer who has come to bribe him for a job for her husband. Even the groan is record rather than adjuration. He is simply amazed that life exists in days, hours and minutes. He is transfixed by wonder at the quotidian of his bodily and working existence, as part of history. He is a man (as Arthur Bryant has said in his well-known Life, which must be read as a companion to the Diary) to whom the most common things were wonderful:

> At night, writing in my Study, a mouse ran over my table, which I shut up fast under my shelfes upon my table till tomorrow. And so home and to bed.

No, he is not addressing a person. He is not even addressing God. It may be that he is addressing history, for he left the Diary to his college at Cambridge: yet the bequest may be due to his passion for preserving papers, for property, an act of vanity in administrative tidiness. No longing for immortality there. If he addressed anything, the future Fellow of the Royal Society was blamelessly addressing the new Curiosity, science itself. It was fashionable to be a Baconian, a virtuoso, to potter on the new outskirts of invention, to catalogue as the Victorian botanists did two centuries later; and this new itch for documentation does strongly influence the diarist as it also influences Defoe. The random private trait comes to life when it is a response to a consciousness of one's times.

Pepys was astutely aware that he was the success thrown up by a revolution which had got rid of its leaders and its dogma and now offered the technologist a fortune: in this he is very modern. The son of a tailor—outside the reactionary Guilds and therefore in the black market—to be shrewd and efficient enough to rise and become the friend of the King! To have erotic dreams about Lady Castlemayne, to become Head of the Navy—and rich! To be the all-powerful valet! Pepys has the essential and topical character of the hero of a picaresque novel like *Gil Blas*. His is the secrecy of the indispensable.

Yet as a careerist and an importance the little man who lets his hair go long is not a bore; he is large and various. His 'morning draught' at the tavern, his drunken evenings, his sing-songs, his playing of the lute, his dancing, his love of pretty well all women, his love of show, the theatre, silver plate; his martinet behaviour with his wife who leaves her clothes on the floor, but whom he adores—a myriad small interests keep him spry. One sees him boring holes into his office wall so that he can spy on his clerks, worried by playing the lute on Sundays, hitting his wife by accident when he wakes up in the morning, boxing his manservant's ears, being forced to leave the Abbey at the high moment of the Coronation because he is bursting to pee. He never misses a public occasion: there is an unmoved account of the execution of Sir Harry Vane. He stayed in London for the plague. His early life in the Admiralty has a low social note which the rising man begins to disapprove—how long a tradition lower-middle-class comedy has!

In the morning to my office, where after I had drunk my morning draught at Will's with Ethell and Mr Stevens, I went and told part of the excise money till 12 o'clock. And then called on my wife and took her to Mr Pierces, she in the way being exceedingly troubled with a pair of new pattens, and I vexed to go too slow, it being late. There when we came, we found Mrs Carrick very fine and one Mr Lucy, who called one another husband and wife; and after dinner a great deal of mad stir; there was pulling off Mrs Bride's and Mr Bridegroom's ribbons, with a great deal of fooling among them that I and my wife did not like; Mr Lucy and several other gentlemen coming in after dinner, swearing and singing as if they were mad; only he singing very handsomely.

Two years later, when he has cut down his oysters and his wine-drinking, moved into a grander house and doubled his time at the office, there is a memorable Sunday, beginning with church, sermon and an excellent anthem and symphony, the organ supported by wind instruments, until:

Thence to My Lord's, where nobody at home but a woman that let me in, and Sarah above, whither I went up to her and played and talked with her and, God forgive me, did feel her; which I am much ashamed of, but I did no more, though I had so much a mind to it that I spent in my breeches. After I had talked an hour or two with her, I went and gave Mr Hunt a short visit, he being at home alone. And thence walked homeward; and meeting Mr Pierce the Chyrurgeon, he took me into Somerset House and there carried me into the Queene-Mother's presence-chamber, where she was with our Queene sitting on her left hand . . . here I also saw Madame Castlemayne and, which pleased me most, Mr Crofts the King's bastard, a most pretty sparke of about 15 years old.

Then the King, the Duke and Duchess came in, 'such a sight as I could never almost have happened to see with so much ease and leisure'. The only thing that worried him on the way home was that he had promised his wife to be there before she got back. Yet he had not done this 'industriously' but by chance. There we have the Puritan, a bit of a cautious rake, a bit of a voyeur, a bit of a romantic snob; but, as he says, his great fault (which he will try and amend) is that he can never say 'No' to anyone. Enormous industry—starting work at four or five in the morning—and temptation are his fate: the Puritan syndrome.

The most absorbing historical part of these three early volumes concerns Pepys's modest, canny but courageous part in the crisis of getting Charles II over, seeing him crowned, and the religious manoeuvres as the Cromwellian revolution was liquidated. Such things in the Diary have been enormously important to historians and there is no more intimate guide to London life at the time. The city streets, taverns, theatres, courts, docks, the business of fitting out ships and paying for it, and political gossip live minutely in the pages. We simply follow in hundreds of journeys down streets or by water to Greenwich, because he is so busy. Why is he so alive, what has given this fat, slightly pompous and fussy little man an edge to his record? Obviously he worked at his desk longer than anyone else in the city, and because of that huge labour we know him. But what made him more than a recorder, and such a recorder? Vitality and curiosity, of course. Three other things are suggestive. First, he had nearly died of the stone when he was very young and he never stopped regarding himself as a miracle because he survived. Maybe—to judge by the case of Montaigne, which perhaps one should not do—the disease has something of the phenomenal in it that encourages a deep physical curiosity. Grave early danger stimulates the appetite for pleasure. Every minute is a gift: catching sight of Lady Castlemayne, 'I glutted myself with looking at her.' Then he was a linguist, which certainly diversifies personality and even offers disguises. The Puritan intensifies his secrecy and his pleasure in using dog-French, Spanish and Dutch in his erotic passages:

nuper ponendo mes mains in su des choses de son breast mais il faut que je leave it lest it bring me alcun major inconvenience.

Finally, in his indiscriminate dabbling in science there is not only his shorthand—the miraculous means of catching life as fast as it flows—but his microscope, which makes life stand still so that it can become as large as life is. Pepys's mind was genial because it was also a microscope. By magnifying, the glass defeated time, it gave an overpowering vividness to memory. Take the example of the ship auction:

> Where pleasant to see how backward men are at first to bid; and yet when the candle is going out, how they bawl and dispute afterwards who bid the most first.
>
> And here I observed one man cunninger than the rest, that was sure to bid the last man and to carry it; and enquiring the reason, he told me that just as the flame goes out the smoke descends, which is a thing I never observed before and by that he doth know the instant when to bid last—which is very pretty.

At night, under his own dying candle, Pepys systematically 'bid last'.

Mr Latham has gone deeply into Pepys's shorthand system and into his methods. His normal prose was the ornate style of the organization man of the period; in the Diary, as if sharing in the Royal Society's new programme for the prose of the new age, he used the plain, rapid, talking language. It catches the instant, saves time and catches time. But were there earlier notes and drafts? There is evidence that there were; that he wrote up the Diary from them days later. (It is known that his famous account of the Fire, which will appear in the later volumes, was done months after the event.) In other words—and this was to be true of Boswell also—the immediacy is in part the effect of revision. Good diaries are good because they are not left in a flabby state of nature, but have been worked on; they are not verbatim or documentary, they are works of art. And to become this they must be obsessional. This was tragically true for Pepys. After eight years he was threatened with blindness. He had to give up the Diary. True he could dictate, but how much he would have to leave out! The only thing was to get the clerk to leave a wide margin in which Pepys could add notes of his own, notes not suited to delicate ears.

'And so', he ends,

> I betake myself to the course which is almost as much as to see myself go into my grave; for which all the discomforts that will accompany my being blind, the good God prepare me.

The human microscope had given up. The snail retired to his official shell.

JONATHAN SWIFT

The Infantilism of Genius

THOSE WHO HAVE read Dr A. L. Rowse's little masterpiece of autobiography *A Cornish Childhood* will guess why that romantic and petulant historian had for over forty years hankered after writing a biographical portrait of Jonathan Swift. An outsider in the political acrimonies of the nineteen-thirties, an early 'Leftist' who has turned against 'Leftist liberal cant', Dr Rowse, in his new book, *Jonathan Swift*, portrays Swift as a fellow-recalcitrant whose ammunition is useful to his biographer in a one-man war against old appeasers and new fanatics: ex-Whig, high Tory, man of crusty commonsense—what could be closer to our combative Cornishman? It is indeed likely that Swift, who hated mankind as a generality but said he loved the individual Jack, William, and Tom, would have found our world third-rate and obscene beyond expression. It is conceivable that Swift would have raged against the appeasement of Hitler, the humbug of Baldwin's England, the errors of the American 'computerwar' in Vietnam, the belief in the educability of everyone, the political fancies of Laputa-like philosophers such as Bertrand Russell, and (of all petty things) even the Value Added Tax, which torments the British of today. (Probably the author of the *Drapier's Letters* would have hated that most.) But when Dr Rowse drags such matters into what is elsewhere a very lucid and moving study of the terrifying Dean of St Patrick's, he reduces him to the level of an irritable writer of letters to *The Times*. To take Swift out of his century is to cloud him and distract us from the incessant pride, passion, and imagination of our supreme satirist and his truly tragic person.

Although Swift struck nearly everyone—especially women
—as the most dazzling, robust, and naturally open man, and
one irresistible in his rudeness, he was deeply secretive and
evasive. His practice of anonymity in his plain, ferocious
writing was not simply a caution before the threats of imprisonment for libel; it was meant to be a momentous
underground game. His exhaustive biographers have found it
impossible to make their minds up about the myths and gossip
that surround his life—and not only because so much of it
comes from Dublin, the most malicious city in Europe. One
half hoped that Dr Rowse would start one of his well-known
hares, but he does not: he ignores, for example, wild stories
like the suggestion that Swift was Sir William Temple's
bastard and the half brother of Stella (Esther Johnson) and
confines himself to what the best scholars have suggested,
sensibly and kindly weighing the possible against the probable.
He bows to Harold Williams and follows Middleton Murry's
much fuller and very feeling *Life*, although, unlike Murry, he
regards Vanessa (Esther Vanhomrigh) as a devouring female
egotist and an impossible plague. As he rather coarsely puts
it, Vanessa was an instance of the unspeakable in pursuit of the
uneatable. Whatever else may be said against the passionate
Vanessa, she was not a fox-hunting girl.

It is agreed that Swift's humiliating failure as a very young
man to persuade Jane Waring (Varina) to marry him set him
violently against marriage for good, and that the words of his
insulting farewell to her hardly suggest that he was impotent.
If we are unlikely to know whether the tale of the secret
marriage to Stella is true, it does seem very possible. Stella
knew Vanessa was in pursuit; she could guess Swift had had
his head turned. Stella's jealousy—and a very rational and
Swift-like poem of hers expresses the feeling with extraordinary and painful detachment—may have made her
insist upon a belated marriage in order to insure her
position; Swift may very well have agreed to it as a

secret trump card to play against Vanessa. We shall never be sure about Scott's tale that Vanessa found out and wrote to Stella, and that in a rage Swift rode out to confront Vanessa with the letter, threw it in her face, and never saw or wrote to her again. The scene is in character—supposing Swift to be a personage in one of Scott's novels. Dr Rowse makes much of the difference in social class between Stella and Vanessa. Once educated by Swift, Stella was well fitted to please in the retired life of clerical society in Ireland. But the gifted Vanessa belonged to fashionable society, which Swift adored, and in training her he made her much more intelligent than the usual run of fashionable women. The core of the comedy, which became a tragedy, is clear in Swift's private poem 'Cadenus and Vanessa', which she allowed to circulate after her death, as a vengeance. The insulting Dean was a practical feminist who in curing his two pupils of female silliness found that his Galateas had perfected their minds but retained their natures. Reason was not all. Stella and Vanessa were rival works of art who came only too powerfully to life when they were fighting for possession of him. His gift for intrigue and self-protection had failed him. What is truly horrible is that after their relatively early deaths, and for reasons of guilt, shame and probably a sexual repression we can only guess at, he became obsessed by the dreadful image of the female Yahoo and the scatological nightmares. Even here we must not be too sweeping. We know that the commonest sight of eighteenth-century streets was excrement; that society stank, and even elegant society was blunt in language; and that one or two men with a skin too few—Smollett, for example—may have revelled in dirt but also, like the scrupulous Dean, preached against it.

If Swift seemed a dull, cold, calculating man—as the bland and censorious Victorians thought—and something of a monster, he was pitiable. If he did not love, he was tender and craved tenderness and cleverness in women. As Dr Rowse says, everything in his life put him apart from other men. His father's death before he was born was surely one decisive factor. That he was kidnapped as a baby in Ireland and taken to England by his nurse, with whom he lived for three years, is strange. That his mother is shadowy and that he was sent away to school at Kilkenny—the best Ireland offered at that time—are pointers to an absolute loneliness. His uncle and cousins could claim connections, but only as poor and distant relations. By the time he was taken in by Sir William Temple at Moor Park, in England, the young egotist was formed. Temple became the father figure to an uncouth boy who had stood on his own in the rough Anglo-Irish world—and what a rough lot the Cromwellian colonists must have been, freed as they were from their native English restraints, their liberty based on stolen land! What heady luck for a clever youth to go to a great English house like Moor Park and find a protector in one of the most cultivated and eminent men in English public life! It was a leap from barbarism to the graces of civilization. What a reinforcement for a poor boy's will to power and ambition! There was a price, of course, and one slowly learned: the great and powerful are wayward and lazy, especially when a difficult young man becomes importunate. Swift wanted spectacular advancement at once; with his eye on the main chance he was disappointed by queens, kings, lords and archbishops throughout his life. The touching thing is that Moor Park became a lasting dream of the good life. When, in a simple, practical way, he persuaded Stella and her companion, Miss Dingley—poor fellow relations—to settle in Dublin after Temple's death he was carrying an imaginary Moor Park in his head.

It strikes one that Swift is an instance of the infantilism of genius: he was a self-regarding child-egotist all his life. The will to instant power may not succeed, but intellectually it is devastating. In a rather schematic inquiry written in the Thirties Mario M. Rossi and Joseph M. Hone have the following words about Swift's egotism which exactly convey his attitude to the great and to Stella and Vanessa:

> From Swift's assertion that he loathed humanity and yet loved Jack, William and Tom we are not to suppose that he loved them for what they were, nor indeed that he had even *knowledge* of them as they were. He loved them in so far as they surrendered to his whim, he loved them for being a sort of extension of himself, other bodies of his overlapping self. He disliked humanity because it was a number of extraneous selves; the egotist cannot identify himself with a mass. He identifies himself with individuals in so far as they are his servants.

In its drastic fashion this seems to me true; one has only to look at Swift's purely practical and self-protective attitude to Stella and Vanessa when emotionally they were in extremis, and indeed when they were dying. The two women loved him in their differing ways and were grateful to him. He was not cold, but—like a child—he was incapable of facing or understanding what *they* felt. And, like a child, he was an expert politician in playing where adults do not play. For example, the baby talk in the *Journal to Stella* so skilfully, to all appearance, addressed to Stella and Miss Dingley for respectability's ingenious sake, is not a lover's baby talk but a brilliant raillery which imitates Stella's lisping habit of speech with everyone when she was a backward child at Moor Park. It is a clever, affectionate, but daring mockery of her childhood, designed to keep her *in statu pupillari*. The baby talk—which he used with no other woman—is, so to say, a juvenile exercise in the art of philandering, at which he was notoriously expert.

Swift's hardness to Stella and Vanessa has often been described as mean, calculating and, at heart, frightened; but, as Dr Rowse can easily show, in Swift's relationship with everyone an exorbitant, ingrained pride—the pride of the solitary who will not give himself—is always there. As an unknown cleric, he forced the great Harley to walk halfway to meet him—not that Harley would notice: he would be either well-mannered or merely drunk in an aristocratic way. Such a pride looks almost insane; it was in fact the source of Swift's genius as a satirist. He did not simply hate; he drew upon all the minutiae that buried hatred makes vivid and effective. It is clear, plain, merry obloquy, as unremitting and unanswerable as a day's rain. What Dr Rowse does not go into—and a biography that makes us feel sympathy for a maimed character may not require this literary comment—is the curious influence of that new fashionable and scientific toy, the magnifying glass, on Swift's imagination. Perhaps that simple instrument played as great a part as pride when he came to assuage his passions in *Gulliver's Travels*. How monstrous or tiny it could make his disgusts or his fears, even his own ego. How right that the elderly child should have written a child's book.

I must say that for the first time in my reading, Dr Rowse has made the factional quarrelling of Queen Anne's London clear and even gripping. We are made to see it and feel it and want to be in it, for the moment, as Swift himself so avidly did. After all, he was trying to stop the slaughter of Marlborough's war. And Dr Rowse is even better on Swift's 'conversion' (if that is the word for it) to Ireland. Hated in Ireland, slandered in Ireland, he became eventually the spokesman for Irish (colonial) liberty—although he despised the Irish for their refusal to help themselves. In one way, little Dublin was just the place for the egotist so passionately and, above all, so pedantically concerned with his own liberty. The city was and is a place where one can exist as an irredeemable personality, giving and receiving blows and becoming notable as a protest at having been born—that splendid Irish grudge. Though Swift was elsewhere regarded as avaricious and as counting every penny, his continual and thoughtful charities in Dublin to those whose needs were real or bizarre made him at one with that charitably uncharitable city, a testy and at last a senile saint.

When one looks back on him again what strikes one is that he recorded the multitude of his daily acts pretty well as closely as Pepys did. He belongs to that very small number of famous people whose daily life is visible to us from hour to hour. That may be, as Rossi and Hone have said, because egotists of Swift's kind have instant passions but no lasting aim, grow tired when there is no one about and turn to telling us even about such silly things as how they get up in the morning.

So I'll rise, and bid you good morrow, my ladies both, good morrow. Come stand away, let me rise: Patrick, take away the candle. Is there a good fire? So—up adazy.

It all comes as sweetly to him as handling a prime minister or terrorizing a duke. The terrible child will play his private games forever, until playing games drives him out of his mind.

RICHARD BURTON

Ruffian Dick

THE BURTONS? THOSE people with the two delinquent
boys who looked like gypsies and who could be seen annoy-
ing the inhabitants of Galway, Boulogne, Tours, Pisa and Pau
in the 1830s. They were the Galway Blazers abroad. There
was father, the Colonel, the soul of honour, pacing up and
down. He had wrecked his career by refusing to give evidence
against Caroline, the wife of George IV. In a family crisis, the
Colonel breaks camp and moves on. The mother? Docile.
The boys? Duellists, beaters-up of tutors and foreign maids,
known to the brothels and the police; fiends, liable to hit out
at their elders if called arch-fiends. They don't like the word
'arch'. (However, later on in life, one of them does get such a
knock on the head that he is dead silent for forty years. One is
sorry and hopes he was not a genius like his brother Richard.)
The West of Ireland, with a lot of eighteenth-century hell-fire
still left in it, perhaps also some delayed Rousseauism, like
Major Edgeworth's, and the colonial precocity, produces in
Richard Burton a noble savage who has brains.

Very early on Richard Burton was uttering Latin in the
Italian style to annoy the English; very early he could speak
Béarnais, French and Italian, a little later, German. All very
well. But one day the Colonel rushes home to find the usual
story of girls and police and learns the boy is dying of fever.
He listens to his snores and says: 'The beast's in liquor.' The
Colonel breaks camp once more. There is some smuggling in
Pau, more duelling and attempts to clip off the opponent's
nose or tonsils in Heidelberg, and then Richard is sent to
Oxford. To him this is the final blow. He takes up with a

gypsy girl in Bagley Wood, learns Romany and reads falconry.
Soon he is sent down to study astrology, alchemy, gambling,
Hindustani and Arabic. Pushed into the Indian Army, he turns
to Gujarati and Persian in Bombay. Languages are a new
appetite. In no time he learns snake-charming from a master,
also hypnotism; he has an Indian mistress, goes in for native
disguises and is known in the mess as 'ruffian Dick' or the
'white nigger'. In a year or two, by the time he is twenty-
eight, he has written two short books of travel, one describing
an attempt to abduct a nun in Goa; another on falconry and a
standard army manual on the bayonet. Then—but this is the
ruin of his military career—a report on pederasty. The General
had asked for it, but had not expected it to be so enthusiastically
complete.

Born today in another class Burton would be in borstal. In
his own period, he is simply an Anglo-Irish Elizabethan, born
out of time. As Mr Farwell, his American biographer, says, he
was a great adventurer rather than one of the great explorers
like Speke, Livingstone or Stanley; he did not make the one
extra and disciplined effort that would get him over the next
hill. At the penultimate moment, on the shores of Tanganyika,
he lacked the obsessive quality of Speke and let this tedious
man go on to discover the source of the Nile.

The odd thing is that though Burton had the Elizabethan
courage and wild, animal energy, he was checked by a taste
that is purely Victorian—the taste for documentation and
cataloguing. He could always be driven on but was always
eventually held up by an appetite for bizarre fact. Indeed
Burton is even less an adventurer than an appetite. He is
Appetite itself. Quarrelsome, autocratic, with no notion of how
to control men on an expedition, Burton was best on his own
where, born mimic and actor that he was, he could disappear
into a disguise and glut his voracity for people, customs and
all physical sights. He is an almost pestiferous pursuer of
whatever can be turned into a footnote. He has no sense of

proportion and therefore no sense of theme. He is always salivating at the news of a detail and there is nowhere he won't stop in order to ask a question. Burton's is an appetite for life not for Nature, though when he is an actor in his surroundings, as he is when riding in the desert, he can describe splendidly. The appetite turns the romantic into a pedant. One has often seen this happen to adventurous men. Alas, his miscellaneous learning did little for his fame; it is only in fairly recent times that he has been recognized as an early anthropologist and that his eccentric 'pornography'—as he was truculently fond of calling it—has been properly instead of improperly appreciated.

If Burton desired Fame, appetite made him neglect the process by which fame is acquired. He would do the dramatic things, like the famous journeys to Mecca and Harar—which are his best—but he just did not bother to rush back home at once with his tale. He was absorbed in his notebooks, filling up more and more of them for his own sardonic pleasure. He enjoyed also what the Arabs call their *Kahl*—just sitting and doing nothing—which, for him, meant derisively scribbling down any fact. It was the hanging around and questioning that kept him at Tanganyika, when he ought—if he wanted Fame—to have gone on.

For an adventurer, Burton is strangely literary and he even has the writer's complacency. When Speke returned to camp after his discovery, Burton fell back on literary egotism and refuted Speke's claim by argument. In Speke's shoes one would have found this intolerable, backed as it was by Burton's bullying and superior airs; one can understand how Speke, a dull, shy man, must have built up a boiling resentment. It was shabby of him to bolt home quickly and claim the credit but the great explorers have usually been great publicity-hunters and sometimes cads; and Burton had only his own intellectual vanity and indolence to blame. One is sorry for the arch-fiend because his total confidence in his power to dominate anybody made him naïve in personal relations: he had no real belief in the existence of anyone but himself.

Burton's sweeping disregard of other people, even when his interests demanded the opposite, is an aspect of his passion for freedom and his love of risk. He had the true adventurer's love of raising the stakes and of imperilling his own situation. In the planning of his journey to Mecca one sees all his virtues and weaknesses at work. He went out to Alexandria disguised in order to train himself thoroughly. As patiently as an actor he studied Moslem behaviour; he perfected his languages; he threw himself into theology and religious observance. He had decided to go as a Persian but, always making casual acquaintances and picking brains, he found out that Sufism was more dangerous than Christianity on this pilgrimage and he switched, in a scholarly way, to the right sect. Irreligious but superstitious, he knew how to dabble successfully in a modicum of faith.

So far, all Burton's thoroughness is evident. Then suddenly—perhaps it was due to the strain or to natural devilment—he risked his plan and his life. On the eve of his departure, he went off on a drinking bout with a lapsed Moslem, and in their cups they tried to force a devout Moslem friend to drink He screamed blue murder. The night was wild and when Burton came round, he had to make a run for it. Again in Mecca, the peril of taking notes was extreme and, like many serious travellers, Burton was a public note-taker. He held himself in but in the end his nature was too much for him. He had the nerve to make a surreptitious scribble in the midst of a religious ceremony, relying on the blindness of ecstasy in the people surrounding him. The trick came off, but he might have been killed on the spot.

When one reads of his adventures—and Mr Farwell's account of them is clear and lively—one realizes that Burton was lucky and that, probably by boldness, made his own luck. His sombre appearance and above all something magnetizing and frightening in his gaze must have given pause when he drew pistols or raised his fists. He had not graduated as a *maître d'armes* in France, nor trained himself as a wrestler, nor written on the bayonet for nothing. He was able to stick terrible physical suffering. He could stand any fever. He had little need of sleep. He could drink like a fish. He created drama or was always at the centre of it. There was something cheerfully appropriate—from Burton's point of view—in the manner of Speke's death. After years of public controversy and accusation, the two antagonists were to meet on a public platform and decide the issue of the Nile once and for all. All was set for the fight—and then Speke couldn't be found. He had shot himself. It was not a suicide but an accident. Burton appears merely to have snorted. In Brazil, Arabia, Beirut or Africa, one had seen deaths just as bizarre as that, and in more interesting circumstances.

And what can have been more bizarre than Burton's marriage? Mr Farwell has nothing new to say about it, but he appreciates the comedy. There was a lot of nonsense in Burton; he was superstitious, he was an actor, his fact-hunting led him to imaginative generalizations about anything. He was very much a man to have his cake and eat it, which meant that his mind delighted in living a double life. On a different level, Isabel Burton matched her nonsense with his. She was infatuated with Burton and the idea of romantic adventure. She was also obstinate. As fast as she filled his pockets with Catholic beads, medals and protective objects, he flung them out of the window. He put *his* faith in horse chestnuts and, during attacks of gout, tied silver coins to his ankle. She made him sign for a Catholic burial; Burton would sign anything, and laughed. What religion had he not had a go at?

The marriage worked very well. And it certainly consoled him in the long period of failure, neglect and defeat that marks his middle life—before at last the gods, if not the British Foreign Office, smiled on him. The gods murmured to him that although he was a failed official, a dull writer, a broken adventurer, there was one more country he could ransack without moving from his room in Trieste. He could rediscover and expound a literature. The translation of the *Arabian Nights* is his most eloquent journey. There, at last, his habit of being distracted from his objective could bear fruit. Let Arabia produce the theme, but leave Burton to add himself and the thousand and one experiences of his life to the Thousand and One Nights.

FREDERICK ROLFE

The Crab's Shell

READING MIRIAM J. BENKOVITZ's life of Frederick Rolfe, who called himself Baron Corvo, one spots in him a Gissing turned inside out. Corvo was all shady personality and Gissing, the real novelist, was scrupulously without it. Their basic resemblance is in original circumstance. Both were lower-middle-class casualties, trained by Puritan poverty for self-righteous failure; both are emotionally arrested or diverted from the norm. Gissing first marries a prostitute and, after, a virago-servant; Corvo is a pederast; both are underdogs. Gissing has no influential friends, Rolfe-Corvo loses his; the pair are naturals for the future of the snubbed hack and the unsaleable 'masterpiece', but are imbued with the pride of the artist-prince which was the cult of *fin de siècle* Bohemia. They belong to the period when the gifted became obsessed with the defeat of aristocracy (i.e. genius) at the hands of Demos, the hooligan mob with its prolific diet, the new popular journalism.

And it is here they part. Gissing the truth-telling realist, drudged and drew directly on the lives around him, though privately he thought of himself as an ancient Greek; Corvo was rigid in his personal dream and quarrelled with those who disturbed it. He cadged a living—also an honorary title from a rich Anglo-Italian patroness—and turned into a small fantastic with a studied Oxford accent. His first eccentric gesture, not without germs of self-interest and pretence, was to turn Roman Catholic and to leave school at fifteen; at twenty-five he began a long struggle to enter the priesthood. His faith seems to have been genuine to the frantic point of pedantry; he became more papist than the Pope and such a prayer-wheel that he was soon at war with his fellow Catholics, high or low. His vision of himself was paranoid: as Miss Benkovitz says more sympathetically, he made the impossible demands of a child in an adult world. He was generally accused of lying and sponging, but if he was continually slapped down by people who were exasperated by him, even reduced to semi-starvation and self-imposed vagrancy, he always rose again indomitably, convinced of himself as a genius and an enterprise. *Hadrian the Seventh* is an inspired piece of vengeful autobiography; and *The Desire and Pursuit of the Whole* a half moving, half absurd psychological give-away. It explains his pederasty: he deeply felt that puberty is a child's most dreadful experience, for the indeterminate wholeness of boyhood and girlhood sex is destroyed. For him, to remain the boy–girl is the only wholeness: he is in a search for complete identity with a friend who embodies this peculiarity.

The quest—as we know from A. J. A. Symons's classic portrait, *The Quest for Corvo*—was fanatical and went floundering into the farcical, the picaresque and finally ended in squalor. Although Miss Benkovitz spells out the story in minute detail and writes very well, I do not think her long book tells us essentially any more than Symons has done, although certain episodes of his career do benefit by expansion; one must grant that the pettifogging of deep neurotics is an important part of their case. And if the detail of Rolfe's dreary and perpetual quarrels as a downtrodden tutor or schoolmaster is tedious, the account of his emotional and financial crushes catches the point that he had a changing image and that he depended, as an actor does, on being seen, heard and talked about. His quarrels also led to amusing changes of company. It is strange to see this man who cultivated archaic prose and speech and who could almost pass as a priest, ghosting a book on African agriculture for a Colonel, flirting with Hugh Bland and E. Nesbit about Socialism—which he detested, but he sent £5 to Bernard Shaw as a contribution to the Fabian Society (hardly the home of the True Church).

Rolfe was a poseur or, more sympathetically, one can say he projected images of himself in which for the time being he idealized and believed. His expectations, once friendship had been given, were preposterous: if he was an adventurer, he really lived or half-lived in the imagination and was self-deluded. When the illusion dissolved because he asked too much he became quarrelsome, litigious and scarifying. His rage at having his vocation denied went deep and by the time he settled down to his notorious Venetian period in middle age, he let himself go.

Miss Benkovitz's skill in threading her way through a minutely entangled story comes into its own as Rolfe-Corvo's life did in Venice. He had called himself variously the Raven, the crab of unbreakable shell, the master of felinity and, after thirty-five years of failure as a writer, his nerve hardened. The sense of 'peerless difference' from other men which he had ingeniously constructed, was now absolute and sustained by long training in a kind of animal cunning. It is not enough to call him a poseur: in Venice he lived the image he had projected. One reason was the beauty of Venice itself; but the private reason was that the twenty years of celibacy required by his attempt to be acceptable to the priesthood had lapsed. He had not lost his faith; he was still ardent in trotting to his prayers. Rome, or rather the clergy and the Catholic laity, had betrayed him. He still had his debts, and his insulting begging letters: he went after the well-off among the English residents and the old story of viciously biting the hand that fed him began once more. But now he was a pagan. His worship of young men and boys was excited by the young gondoliers. He had always kept himself strong by exercises, but now he became an oarsman on the canal; the young gondoliers were his friends and teachers. He had his own little boat in which he would sleep out in the winter, plagued by the rats of the canals, when he was evicted from his lodgings or dropped as intolerable by the residents. He was writing *The Desire and Pursuit of the Whole* and caricatured his benefactors. Of one, a long-suffering Dr Van Someren, he wrote that he was dishonest in mind, a bore and a hypocrite. His savaging of this dietician is very funny: 'I never want to see your food-splashed face again, you have had your chance and you have mucked it up most magnificently.'

But if there were months of desperation, Rolfe-Corvo went on with his literary work in his painfully beautiful handwriting, and there are an adventurer's spells of fortune. At one time he had a gondola equipped with sails on which he had painted crabs and ravens, a heraldic device at the prow and 'a great Saint George (a Perseus–Poseidon–Hermes kind of nudity) at the poop'. It was lined with the skins of leopards and lynxes and was handled (John Cowper Powys wrote) by 'a Being who might have passed as a faun', while at rest upon the leopard skins lay Corvo, 'one of the most whimsical of writers'. That was glory. But the notorious Venice Letters written by Rolfe to Masson Fox between 1909 and 1910 tell the story of moral disintegration which shocked A. J. A. Symons. They appear to show Rolfe as a pimp, enticing a pederast, offering to supply boys; and one letter describes what purports to be one of his own sexual encounters. As Miss Benkovitz says, there is a case for thinking Rolfe was chaste but that, if this is not accepted, then the Letters are in fact pornographic letters designed to entice by imagined accounts of lust, and are a disguised form of begging. This, knowing his skill and history, they may very well be. What they do reveal, as she says, is the 'rampant sexuality' of a man living in his imagination. How can one tell? One can only note that his chief gift as a writer was his visual power, his invention of startling if affected images. He is a man for sensations and the physical surfaces—not for nothing had he started life as a photographer, colourer of photographs and designer of emblems—as this random example from

Hadrian the Seventh shows when he writes that the Pope's voice: 'was a cold white candent voice which was more caustic than silver nitrate and more thrilling than a scream.'

Miss Benkovitz's *Life* does not claim to be a critical biography and, as she says, there can be no complete understanding of Rolfe without an examination of the work in relation to his period. Still she tells one enough. It is a matter of taste, but for myself the affectations and insinuations of his Huysman-like world have no appeal. One has the impression of surfeit, fake and even of hysteria loitering in the wings. I have read no more than *Hadrian the Seventh*. It is dashing in its semi-learning. For a man who was rejected by the Church in which he saw his salvation, to hit upon the notion that he has, in proper fashion, been elected Pope and is sought out by the crowned heads of Europe is brilliant. And, at any rate in the early chapters, the book is ingeniously convincing in all its sardonic detail. Rolfe had an actor's detachment from his own character and played many parts with an effrontery which amounts to courage. The weakness of *Hadrian the Seventh* as a chronicle is that it eventually becomes a shrewd journalist's 'think-piece'. Still, as we know, the boldness of the fantasy is excellent pantomime. How far away we are from the sight of poor self-pitying Gissing turning out the blameless papers of Henry Ryecroft by the Ionian Sea, and mildly wishing he was a respectable ancient Greek, yet a writer far more diverse, and fuller than Rolfe-Corvo ever was.

LADY MURASAKI

The Tale of Genji

WHEN ARTHUR WALEY's translation of *The Tale of Genji*
came out, volume by volume, in the late Twenties and early
Thirties, the austere sinologue and poet said that Lady Murasaki's work was 'unsurpassed by any long novel in the world'.
If we murmured, 'What about *Don Quixote* or *War and Peace*?'
we were, all the same, enchanted by the classic of Heian Japan
which was written in the tenth and eleventh centuries, and we
talked about its 'modern voice'. What we really meant was
that the writing was astonishingly without affectation. Critics
spoke of a Japanese Proust or Jane Austen, even of a less coarse
Boccaccio. They pointed also to the seeming collusion of the
doctrines of reincarnation or the superstition of demonic
possession with the Freudian unconscious—and so on.

Arthur Waley admitted a remote echo of Proust, for there
was a nostalgia for *temps perdu* in a small aristocratic civilization; but he was quick to point out that the long and rambling
Tale was hardly a psychological novel in the Western sense.
The Chinese had excelled in lyrical poetry, but despised fiction
outside of legend and fairy tale; in Japan, Lady Murasaki's
contemporaries were given only to diarizing. What she had
contrived was an original mingling of idealizing romance and
chronicle, but a more apt analogy was with music: the effect
of her classical and elegant mosaic suggested the immediate,
crystalline quality of Mozart. Evocations of instrumental
music and also of things like the music of insects occur on page
after page: at one point Genji floods a garden with thousands
of crickets. The more one thinks about this, one sees that

Waley's insight contains a truth: it is music that steps across the one thousand years that separate us from Lady Murasaki.

A translator like Waley would have European reasons for thinking her 'modern': Japanese art had played its part in the revolution that was occurring in European painting—see Van Gogh, and Picasso in the early 1900s—and English prose was ceasing to be Big Bow Wow. Both the sententious and the precious were yielding to the personal, the conversational, the unofficial, the unaffected, and the fantastic—one sees this in Forster and, above all, in Virginia Woolf, who had contrived an ironical mingling of the formal and natural. Such a change reflects the moment when a culture reaches a sunset in which private relationships are given supreme importance and when there is leisure for wit and perspective and an intense sensibility to the arts for their own sake.

I think this may go some way to explain why the post-1914 period in England produced admirable translations like Waley's, Beryl de Zoëte's *Confessions of Zeno* (which may have improved on the regional prose of Trieste, but captured the marked Viennese spirit of the original), Scott Moncrieff's Proust, and Constance Garnett's Chekhov and Turgenev. Their translations are gracefully late-Edwardian, and are, of course, metaphors; the translators felt an affinity of period, even though (as we are now told by critical scholars) they made serious mistakes or generalized and embroidered in such a way as to mislead. Since translators are bound to work in images, and not only sentence by sentence but paragraph by paragraph or page by page, generalizations tend to drift off course, and in some translators, the act of re-creation, though often inspired, is not self-effacing.

As both poet and scholar, Arthur Waley has often been suspected of re-inventing with the wilfulness of the poet. He was never in China or Japan: his enormous knowledge was that of the hermit of the British Museum. The generation that followed him are far from any *belle époque* and are dedicated technicians strictly bound to their texts. Professor Edward G. Seidensticker, an American scholar, belongs to this school. In his translation of *The Tale of Genji* he tells us that he owes his admiration for the *Tale* to Waley's often wonderful translation and says that Waley often genuinely improved on the original (with one or two exceptions) by drastic cutting when the book bored him. It has its *longueurs*. Seidensticker's chief criticism of Waley is that he embroidered (as an admirer of Virginia Woolf might well do), that his language is far less laconic than the original Japanese, and that, more seriously, he did not catch the rhythm of Japanese prose. I would guess on re-reading Waley that this may be true. Seidensticker's translation, which gives the whole uncut, is still shorter than Waley's! There was indeed a languor in his prose.

It is impossible to do more than point out a few of the 800 characters of the story which passes from episode to episode. The main dramas move among the large number of Genji's love affairs, which are as various as those in Boccaccio. Princes and their trains move from the capital, where all is ambition and court gossip, to the country, where mysterious girls, usually of noble connection, have been hidden, protected only by corruptible or sentimental nuns or servants. There are soldiers but they do not fight. There is no violence. There are no crimes of passion. There are a few rather unpolished provincial governors—a despised caste. Lady Murasaki is as sensitive as Jane Austen is to rank and status, noting drily the pretentious who have come to nothing and the common who have risen. There are priests in their temples, soothsayers, exorcists who are called in to throw out demons, which are, as a rule, projections of jealous passion.

We see a society ruled by ceremonies and rituals and checked by taboos. Ill-luck, bad behaviour, tragedy may be caused in one's life by influences from a previous incarnation for which one cannot be held responsible. Lady Murasaki's temperament is not religious: for her, religion is a matter of proper observances and manners. She has a taste for funerals properly conducted.

The sexual act is never described; the ecstasies of physical love are not even evoked conventionally as they are rather tiringly in *The Arabian Nights*. We see the lovers meet with a screen between them. They strike the string of the koto or exchange short poems to show their artistic skills. The touching of an embroidered sleeve causes alarm and desire; when the lover is admitted or breaks in, the servants retire and we have a full description of the lady's clothes and her hair, but not her body. A coverlet is removed and the next thing we know is that night has passed and the lover is required to leave at dawn under cover of the perpetual mist, his sleeves washed by the dews. He hands the lady a sprig of blossom and sends her a two-line poem with a conversational postscript. The book is almost entirely concerned with the interplay of feelings, joyful, sorrowing, and longing. All is rendered with classical restraint.

The magnificent and always engaging Genji dominates two-thirds of the book and then with little explanation fades out of it. (Perhaps the manuscript has been lost.) He is incurably susceptible and unfaithful, but he makes amends to his conscience by behaving generously. Society deplores but forgives what are called 'his ways'. He is the illegitimate and favourite son of the emperor—'a private treasure'—and he is scarcely more than a boy when he falls in love with his stepmother, the emperor's second wife, who seems, in this incestuous society, to be an ideal. She has a child by him, but that is nothing. He is married off to Aoi, another woman years older than himself. They do not cohabit and she treats him like a schoolboy but in time he will love her deeply. Meanwhile he takes Lady Rokujō, his uncle's wife, also many years older than himself, as his mistress.

Lady Rokujō's violent jealousy of Aoi leads to one of the great dramatic scenes of the book, for if she is resigned to

Genji's casual love affairs, she finds his love of Aoi intolerable. The drama comes to a head at the Festival of Kamo. An enormous crowd of all classes comes to see the nobility ride by on horseback. There is a great traffic jam of fine carriages, among them Aoi's. Lady Rokujō has gone incognito to the festival in a simple curtained carriage, to get one last glimpse of Genji, but her carriage and her attendants collide with Aoi's. There is a brawl between the rival servants and Lady Rokujō is pushed into the background.

The affront is devastating. From now on the evil spirit of jealousy becomes a demonic entity. Aoi is pregnant, indeed about to give birth, and is found to be dying. The evil spirit has indeed entered her, and when the demented Genji speaks to her, she answers in the voice of Lady Rokujō. Powerless to control herself Lady Rokujō has projected her voice into the dying woman. It is an instance of possession. Such scenes are not uncommon in romance, but this one is so well done that we believe it and feel the horror. A wild emotion has been transmitted and is recognizable as an emanation of the unconscious, for Lady Rokujō, who has not consciously willed this act, nevertheless feels remorse. It drains her of all desire to continue her powerful life at court: to annul the magic that possesses her she enters a nunnery. Had the scene been done in the high manner of romance it would be as unreal as a fairy tale; in fact the writing is restrained and therefore frightens us.

Genji's 'ways' continue rashly until he sins against protocol and is obliged to go into exile in the mountains. The whole court, even the offended emperor, is upset. There are many rough journeys over muddy tracks, in fog, snow, freezing winds, across flooded rivers. The amount of rain that pours down in the *Tale* must be about equal in volume to the floods of tears, whether of joy, grief, longing, or remorse, which so easily overcome the characters. The tears themselves are a kind of music, a note of the koto. In exile, Genji thinks of his new wife, Murasaki—she seems unlikely to have been the authoress—and of his other ladies. But Genji cannot really repent. He thinks of old lovers:

> He went on thinking about whatever woman he encountered. A perverse concomitant was that the women he went on thinking about went on thinking about him.

A cuckoo calls—it is a messenger from the past or the world beyond death, not the mocking creature of Western culture.

> It catches the scent of memory, and favours
> The village where the orange blossoms fall.

Even the sinister Lady Rokujō is forgiven. She had been a woman of unique breeding and superior calligraphy. She replies in a long letter:

> Laying down her brush as emotion overcame her and then beginning again, she finally sent off some four or five sheets of white Chinese paper. The gradations of ink were marvellous. He had been fond of her, and it had been wrong to make so much of that one incident. She had turned against him and presently left him. It all seemed such a waste.

The lady of the orange blossoms, an older mistress, writes:

> Ferns of remembrance weigh our eaves ever more,
> And heavily falls the dew upon our sleeve.

A Gosechi dancer, a wild girl, writes:

> Now taut, now slack, like my unruly heart,
> The tow rope is suddenly still at the sound of a koto.
> Scolding will not improve me.

Genji spends his time among the fishermen of the wild Akashi coast and here, of course, temptation comes and he is sending messages to a girl hidden in one of the houses, a rustic, whose parents have 'impossible hopes'. Her father is a monk, but soon stops his prayers when he sees Genji may raise her fortunes. Genji admires beyond the protecting screen:

Though he did not exactly force his way through, it is not to be imagined that he left matters as they were. . . . The autumn night, usually so long, was over in a trice.

No hope of a respectable marriage for her. All the same, Genji will install her in the capital later in the story and she will have her influence on his life. As usual, he is guilty about this secret. The girl had enhanced his love of his wife, to whom he confesses.

It was but the fisherman's brush with the salty sea pine
Followed by a tide of tears of longing.

His wife replies gently but ironically, in words that have a bearing on the Calderón-like theme of the novel, i.e. that life is a dream:

That you should have deigned to tell me a dreamlike story which you could not keep to yourself calls to mind numbers of earlier instances.

And politely adds to her poem:

Naïve of me, perhaps; yet we did make our vows.
And now see the waves that wash the Mountain of Waiting.

She knows that Genji will not stand jealous scenes for one moment. Everyone knows it. His lasting defence of his adding new loves to old is that he never forgets, and he adds: 'Sometimes I feel as if I might be dreaming and as if the dream were too much for me': it is an attempt to define what life itself, with all its happiness and disasters, feels like.

Genji's early love of mother figures perhaps necessarily accounts for the incestuous strain in him. His second wife (i.e. Murasaki) was taken into his mansion as a child and he has brought her up to think of him as her father. He flirts with the little girl; then, when she reaches puberty, he can't control himself and gets into bed with her. It is a kind of rape. The girl is shocked and sullen. The silent aftermath is plainly and delicately shown; but ritual saves the situation. The required offerings of cakes are pushed through her bed curtains. Marriage follows and, in time, she adores him. She has after all married the ruler of the country; however, in years to come, she will find him playing the father game again. He has by this time installed his chief concubines in apartments in his mansion; each has her own superbly made garden. He is getting on—probably in his forties—and he likes dropping in for a chaste evening chat with some of the older ones. There is some discreet bitching among the women, disguised as two-edged gardening presents. One older lady sends the younger Murasaki an arrangement of autumn leaves with the words:

Permit the winds to bring a touch of autumn.

Murasaki's garden is without flowers at this time. She replies with an arrangement of moss, stones, and a cleverly made artificial pine, with the words:

Fleeting, your leaves that scatter in the wind.
The pine at the cliffs is forever green with the spring.

The pine is a symbol of hopeless longing and Genji tells his wife she has been 'unnecessarily tart'.

'What will the Goddess of Tatsuta think when she hears you belittling the best of autumn colours? Reply from strength, when you have the force of your spring blossoms to support you.'

The magnificent man is fortifying because he is not only benevolent by nature, but also astute.

After the deaths of Genji and his second wife, the novel is dominated by a new generation: Yūgiri, Genji's pompous son, and the young heroes and courtiers, Niou and Kaoru. These two are friends, who laugh and drink together, and also rivals. The important thing is the marked difference of their temperaments, and on this Lady Murasaki becomes searching. Niou is the handsome and dashing Don Juan or playboy who lacks Genji's powers of reflection. Kaoru has a startling physical quality. In a story where the men are known by the scent they use, Kaoru has a body that needs none: its natural fragrance can intoxicate 200 yards away like the smell of some powerful flower. (It can of course betray where he has been!) If this perfume allures it does him no good: he is a neurotic, tormented, indecisive, and self-defeating Puritan who botches his feelings and escapes into the fuss of court administration at the decisive moment. Responsibility is his alibi and curse. The explanation of his insecure character is that he is a bastard incurably depressed because he does not know who his father is.

The rivalry between Niou and Kaoru begins with a long intrigue with two orphaned sisters who live in the Uji country, a solitude of howling winds and sad rivers. Elsewhere we hear the cheeping of the crickets, the songs of birds, but at Uji the music is the mournful, deafening, maddening music of waterfalls. Niou quickly conquers one of the sisters but only to make her his concubine and not his wife. Kaoru, who is in love with both girls, in his way, loses both. His trouble is that he is an intellectual whose real interest is religion. He will eventually take the vows of Buddhism.

The 'novel' has by now almost ceased to be a work of worldly and poetic comedy and, in its last part, becomes a fast moving drama of intrigue and passion and dementia in which lying servants and old women play their part. (The analogy is extravagant, I know, but it is as if we had moved from, say, Jane Austen to an Oriental version of *Wuthering Heights*.) This final section, along with the opening one of the *Tale*, is by far the most gripping. It excited Arthur Waley! The drama arises from one more adventure of the rivals. Niou and Kaoru are this time in love with a simple, hidden girl of mysterious parentage called Ukifune. Kaoru loves her because she reminds him of the one he had lost earlier—memory, or being reminded of earlier loves, is a continuous musical theme— Niou is out for yet another rash seduction.

The girl is too young to know who of the two she loves and who is her friend; and in her misery decides to drown herself as girls always do, Lady Murasaki remarks, in the romances she has read. The girl attempts this and disappears, and is generally supposed to be dead. Indeed the servants arrange a false funeral in order to avoid scandal. They go out with a coffin containing her bedding and clothes, and burn them on the funeral pyre; the country people, who take death seriously, are suspicious and shocked by the hurry. They watch the smoke: it smells of bedding, not of a burning corpse. In fact, unknown to Niou and Kaoru and ourselves, Ukifune has been rescued and hidden once more in a temple. We see Niou shocked by grief for the first time in his life. (Lady Murasaki is remarkable in scenes of wild grief.) The extraordinary thing is her account of Ukifune's loss of memory and speech after the 'drowning': it is done with astonishing realism and could be a clinical study.

Lady Murasaki is almost too inventive. She is, as I have said, properly class-conscious, quick to detect the vulgar, and is therefore capable of refreshing bits of farce. Pushing, common provincial governors or tomboys with bad accents are neatly hit off: 'Pure, precise speech can give a certain distinction to rather ordinary remarks,' she notes like any lady in a Boston or London drawing room, *circa* 1910. Girls who talk torrentially become 'incomprehensible and self-complacent'. Still, eventually there is a chance that being in good society will cure them. On the other hand, don't imagine that there is any deep difference between the aristocrat and the lowborn: the sorrows of life afflict all. Life is short, time swallows us up; old palaces fall into ruins, new ones take their place. Our life is a dream and, like the *Tale* itself, fades away.

As a translator Seidensticker matches Waley's excellence in detail: theirs is a ding-dong rivalry. There are Anglo-American differences in talk and if Seidensticker's manner is laconic this sometimes runs him into the heavily jaunty word. (Look back to that phrase 'perverse concomitant' in my earlier quotation.) There are many amusing episodes in Seidensticker which are missing from Waley: on the other hand one grasps the whole more easily from Waley's discursive pages even if he is artfully generalizing.

In his preface Waley has more to say by way of literary judgment in his stern, sensitive manner; Seidensticker's preface is more informative about the peculiar history of the manuscripts and composition, and about Lady Murasaki herself. It is curious that literary work of this kind was solely an occupation for women in her time, and Seidensticker thinks that this may be because unlike the women of other Oriental cultures Japanese women were free of harem politics; also that they were less conventional than the men, who were tied to the bureaucracy and the endless ceremonies of the court. Lady Murasaki's contemporaries were simply diarists; she was widowed early. Perhaps, in loneliness, she took the leap from memoir into the imagination, and, looking back, felt that 'the good life was in the past': this indeed is the meaning of Genji's name.

RUTH PRAWER JHABVALA

Snares and Delusions

RUTH PRAWER JHABVALA'S stories have been compared to
Chekhov's. She is a detached observer of what he called *morbus
fraudulentus*, the comedy (in the sternest sense) of self-delusion
which leaves us to make up our minds. Her novel *A New
Dominion* embodies this irony, but one is more struck, this
time, by the echoes of *A Passage to India*. Two generations have
passed since Forster. The Westerner is not now in India to
rule or give. He is either an apologetic foreign official, a tourist
safe in his hygienic hotel, seeing the sights but fearful of
their implications, or—more rarely—a 'seeker' in flight from
the materialism of the West who is confused by the materialism of the East. But, allowing for this difference, Forster's
and Mrs Jhabvala's characters are matched. Raymond, the
sensitive English aesthete and inquirer, is another Fielding,
plus unconscious homosexuality; his Indian friend, the in-
genuous and plaguing student Gopi, is a budding, ill-educated,
up-to-date version of Dr Aziz. The disturbance in the mind of
the unhappy Mrs Moore becomes bold and explicit in the
persons of three English girls who have recklessly gone to
India on a spiritual quest. They throw themselves without
defence upon India in order to attain their 'higher selfhood'
and to find their 'deepest essence'. To these lengths Forster's
characters never went, for the girls have come to suffer, to be
destroyed so that they can be remade. Times have changed,
but the theme is similar: opposites have met.

In one way, Mrs Jhabvala's book is a satirical study of the
disasters that overtake those who dabble in the wisdom of the
East, and one can think the lesson forced. The girls are rootless,

daring, and sexually frigid. One is told little about their background. Under what circumstances in their native land did
these virgins, or demi-virgins, pick up the idea of something
'higher' than sexual love? Why, one asks, didn't they become
nuns at home? Or are they in some sense hippies? We do not
know. And are these three not too alike? The Western
characters in *A New Dominion* are denatured types. Raymond
has collected his scholarly information and firmly saves his
skin with Gopi's mockery in his ears: 'Sometimes you are just
like a woman. Look how neat you are and tidy!' For the girls—
disaster, though they are trite until disaster catches them. One
of them dies of hepatitis and in squalor, because her chosen
swami disbelieves in modern medicine. Another has become a
pale, glazed automaton, the swami's hypnotized slave: the
most truthful and stubborn of the three girls holds onto her
Western will. But against her judgment and despite what she
has seen, she abandons herself to a sexual experience that
disgusts, terrifies and overpowers her. She craves to be
dominated against her will. She has, indeed, discovered an
unsuspected self—one compelled by horror. She finds 'wholeness' in degradation, a craving not for the highest but for the
lowest—and with her eyes open.

Yet if Mrs Jhabvala's novel is in part satirical, it rises above
satire in her patient, sensitive, and undismayed treatment of
the situation. Her attitude is that of the careful truth-teller
rather than of the arguer; the irony lies between the honest
lines, so if we feel that the girls are bickering shadows and
their behaviour is unbearably silly and pretentious, they are
always explicit when, from time to time, they come on the
scene. The inner subject of the book is the idea of dominion. In
the foreground is the dominion of the new, rich, brash, Indian
middle class, itself torn between the dominion of its traditions
and the vulgar, careless ostentation now available to it.
Sexuality will dominate, luxury will dominate, the gurus will
dominate, squalor will dominate, servants will intrigue and be

downtrodden. Yet all have their eager, dreamy eyes on the West. The girls are dominated less by the swami than by his insinuation of his belief in Fate: India, in its chaos, has its ancient belief in the domination of Fate in its bones. This is exactly the theme for Mrs Jhabvala, who probably knows more about India and *feels* it more strongly, in terms of personal conflict, than any other novelist writing in English. She has a constant power of collecting the scene in hundreds of glittering fragments—the life of Delhi, Benares, and a desert province—and of losing herself in the contradictions and ambiguities of temperament. Her prose has not the plain Chekhovian transparency, but her method is one that curbs pure satire, for the novel is built up from dozens of short passages in which each character speaks for himself. A large number of these passages are short stories in which the light changes from the bizarre to the poetic, from the comic to the horrifying, from the thoughtful to the mischievous—all with an allusiveness, a susceptibility to mood, a tenderness of which Chekhov was the exemplar. The light in which we see the people, and in which they see each other, changes every minute.

The Hindus are Mrs Jhabvala's complete characterizations—above all, the ancient Princess Asha and the impossible young Gopi. Under their impetuosity they have reserves of cynicism and passivity, and they have no dramatic notions of being 'remade' by their 'saints' and gurus. They run to them with a gambler's abandon; they are stroked, cuddled, bullied, starved into a passing repentance, until at last boredom sets in, and then off they go, to sin with greater carelessness or battered desperation. The gurus are simply islands in a flood of uncontrolled emotion. The Princess seduces Gopi out of hand, though he is a mere youth. She will never cease to be sensually frantic, unscrupulous, disorderly in her jealousy, and avid for the Western gin bottle as she heaves gorgeously on her divan, either caressing or in tears. She is also a wily judge of human nature. She will never believe that the delusions of sensual love and the delight in being adored are not worth it. When Gopi is sentenced to a traditional marriage, she is in despair, but after a spell with her 'saint' she realizes that a maternal love of the young man can be a new refinement of Eros. And Gopi, after observing his Westerners, concludes that, narrowed by guilt, they know nothing of the amusing varieties of the sexual impulse. It is true that Gopi is a boaster of little accomplishment, but he is uninhibited.

The Princess is a remarkable mixture of the blowsily vulgar and the distinguished. She loves to behave atrociously at her adored brother's house—he is a rich and rising politician—and, out of jealousy, to outrage her high-minded sister-in-law, who is a stern Gandhian. The Princess always provides comedy. In their gardens, her brother and his wife stage a grand party and the very proper guests are brought out to sing Gandhian hymns. They walk out onto the moonlit lawns:

Led by the Lady Minister, they had begun to sing hymns. They started off with Gandhiji's favourite hymn—a rousing tune and heartening words about the Oneness of God whether worshipped as Ishwar or as Allah. Unfortunately most of the guests did not know these words and they trailed behind the leader, who sang in a loud and manly voice, sometimes clapping her hands to rally the others along. They kept tripping up and some of them giggled at their own ineptitude, which made others sing louder in order to cover up. They sounded terrible.

Gopi is there. He has sneaked away from Asha in order to flirt with a girl who is as pretty as an ornament. Asha has got together a rival group of musicians who are far from being hymn singers: they represent the old, wicked, malicious India, which insinuates its power through the senses:

The tabla player had now begun to accompany the maestro, and they were working themselves up to a contest where each tried to outwit the other with superior skill. The sitar flung a phrase of unmatchable beauty towards the tabla which responded by not only matching but even surpassing it so that the sitar was forced to try again: and so they continued to cap triumph with triumph, challenging one another to soar higher and higher and up to heaven if possible. Each of them secretly smiled to himself, and sometimes they also exchanged smiles in a mischievous way for each knew what pride there was in the other's heart.

The hymn singers are forced to stop and, to complete the rout of the Lady Minister's respectable party, Asha rushes forth in a fury to drag Gopi away by the hair. Afterwards, she has one of her bouts of shame—shame itself being a luxury—and goes to see an old 'saint' she has known. But her aged servant strokes her forehead and sings her folk songs about the thighs of heroic lovers and secret passages to the bedroom. The ancient mischief of India undermines Asha's calm and revives her passions. Soon she is back with Gopi and the gin in a pleasure palace that had belonged to her old rip of a father—a place that has known all kinds of love and even murder.

Gopi is an intolerably crude yet touching young man, childishly moody and tiresome in his insecurity. He at once tempts, mocks and envies the prim Raymond who may not be willing to consider the nature of his attachment but has the strength of his inhibitions. He watches Gopi's antics with remarkable detachment and tolerance. Gopi fingers Raymond's clothes and furniture greedily; his hands covet any Western object. He has a shameless eye for the main chance. He likes to dress up, to envy, and to annoy. He passionately longs for friendship, yet is negligent in return. He makes scenes about the superiority of his feelings to anything a Westerner can match, yet he is as coarse and egotistical as a child. He is the kind of character (but this is true of everyone in the novel) who is best seen episodically, and in brief scenes Mrs Jhabvala is excellent. Each episode is framed in a passing aspect of the Indian scene: the heat of the day, the sweetness of the evening, the fears of the night, the squalid, the brutal, the absurd. And one is made to feel the tension of the senses. In Benares, while Raymond and Gopi are being rowed on the river by a worn-out old man, Gopi sings a sad love lyric:

> As soon as he was out on the water [Raymond] felt as if all the squalor of the city—the stale puddles, the rotting vegetables, the people waiting to die on the sidewalks—was all suddenly purified and washed away. Yet how could that be? How could that water purify anything? Crowds of people, many of them diseased, were constantly dipping into it—and not only living people but even the remnants of dead bodies which (on account of poverty and the high cost of wood) had not been burned up completely. But Raymond, especially with Gopi sitting opposite him singing his lyric, found it easy to ignore these facts.

Yet the contentment vanishes as they glide into one more raw scene with Asha.

All Mrs Jhabvala's scenes are so ingeniously put together that the wry, the absurd and even the terrible mingle in the space of a few minutes. One situation bears upon another, and all the more sharply because the speakers rarely answer one another but pursue what is going on in the isolation of their own minds. India is indeed evoked by non-communication. To take one outstanding example: when Raymond, in his best moral form, is trying to make Asha give up Gopi because of his coming marriage, arguing that the boy will get bored and leave her, Asha cunningly tells him of the suicide attempt of a young man who went further than Raymond has ever dared to go. In this she is covertly needling him about his repressed feelings for Gopi. Raymond counters that manoeuvre by saying primly, 'Asha, I don't think I need to hear this.' While they talk, the incurable Gopi is playing a raucous Western record on a tinny gramophone and trying to transpose it to an Indian scale as he sings. It sounds awful, and he laughs at himself. The incident ends abruptly:

> Raymond said: 'You really shouldn't make him drink so much. He's not used to it'.
> 'If you take him away, I don't know what I shall do. Can you imagine being alone here?'
> 'You don't have to stay here'.
> She said, 'It's the same everywhere. In Bombay too. Those sounds you say you hear at night, so often I hear them in Bombay. Of course I know it's the sea, really, but to me it sounds like here and then I think I am here'.

What are these sounds? They are the screams of the hyenas. Heavy, dark birds hang motionless in the sky above them.

One can see why the comparison with Chekhov has been made. Like so many of the Russians, Mrs Jhabvala 'made it strange' and has caught hours of the passing day through the comedies and tragedies of her people, especially the Indians. The hour is her measure. With her Englishman and her English girls, Forsterism comes in. Here I find her schematic, for they are outside the Indian hour; they are arguments of young and baffled shadows in a novel where the vitality is elsewhere.

FLANN O'BRIEN

Flann v. Finn

FLANN O'BRIEN AND Myles na Gopaleen (Myles of the Little Ponies) were among the pen names disguising the comic genius of a Dublin civil servant called Brian O'Nolan who became celebrated in 1939 for the 'novel' *At Swim-Two-Birds*, the finest piece of learned comic fantasy to come out of Dublin since the Treaty. Despite the praise of James Joyce, Graham Greene, Anthony Burgess, John Updike and Dylan Thomas—the last said it was 'just the book to give your sister if she's a loud, dirty, boozy girl'—the book did only moderately well. Its successor, *The Third Policeman*, did not find a publisher in Flann O'Brien's lifetime. He turned to journalism, as Myles na Gopaleen, with a satirical column in the *Irish Times* entitled *Cruiskeen Lawn* (*The Little Overflowing Jug*). He wrote a parody in Irish, *The Poor Mouth*, and, among other things, the well-known *Dalkey Archives* which was turned into a ribald play, one of whose characters is St Augustine: he is discovered underwater off the Irish coast. After O'Brien's death in 1966, at the age of fifty-four, *The Third Policeman* at last appeared.

Flann O'Brien was a fierce, elusive and legendary figure in a city where people become legends very rapidly and bitter gossip is much admired. He seemed to inhabit a wide-brimmed black hat and disappeared and reappeared, dissolving his anger, sorrows and learning in whisky and black porter. When, a year before he died, I was told I'd probably meet him somewhere on the street between O'Connell Street and Trinity, he seemed to me to be a vapour. We stood in the usual drizzle. His voice was soft and courteous, he had a look of pride and shy appeal in his small reddened eyes. Then he vanished: goodness knows where; down the Quays or into oblivion among his illnesses?

Now, as one can tell from *A Flann O'Brien Reader*, edited by Stephen Jones, he has an international fame. This book has the admitted disadvantage of being a collection of extracts from his chief works, but it does give a tang of masterpieces like *At Swim-Two-Birds* and *The Dalkey Archives*. Mr Jones's introductions are a help in a discursive way; they contain also a number of O'Brien's anxious letters to his publishers and some biographical hints. As a family, the O'Nolans seem to have had the advantage of a rambling literary education in Latin, Greek and Gaelic, which sharpened their appetite for 'the word' and the distractions of haphazard learning. When I say 'rambling' I must add that at University College O'Brien did take a master's degree with a thesis on Nature in modern Irish poetry. His gentle and serious evocations of Nature are very delicate. The following sentence recalls the medallion-like landscapes in P. G. Wodehouse: 'The whole overhead was occupied by the sky, translucent, impenetrable, ineffable and incomparable, with a fine island of cloud anchored in the calm two yards to the right of Mr Jarvis's outhouse.' The comic spirit is poetic at heart.

Naturally Flann O'Brien is seen in Dublin as an heir to Joyce: nowadays critics talk of Beckett, Borges, Barth, Queneau, the *nouveau roman*, and the anti-novelists who breed fiction out of other fictions. We take the point, but this process was well known to ancient cultures like the Gaelic and, indeed—for the English contributions to Irish writing—to the Elizabethans, not to mention Sterne, who was brought up in Ireland. O'Brien's domestic desuetude and Rabelaisian innuendo are pure *Tristram Shandy*:

Aren't you very fond of your bedroom now, my uncle continued. Why don't you study in the dining-room here where the ink is and where there is a good bookcase for your books?

Boys but you make a great secret about your studies. . . .

My bedroom is quiet, convenient and I have my books there. I prefer to work in my bedroom, I answered. . . . I know the studying you do in your bedroom, said my uncle. Damn the studying you do in your bedroom.

I denied this.

Nature of denial: Inarticulate, of gesture.

Amid belchings, scratching the lice on his person and recovering from a drinking 'bash', the young student narrator of *At Swim-Two-Birds* lies on his grubby bed discussing literature with a friend called Brinsley:

The entire corpus of existing literature should be regarded as a limbo from which discerning authors could draw their characters as required, creating only when they failed to find a suitable existing puppet. The modern novel should be largely a work of reference. . . .

That is all my bum, said Brinsley.

The student then holds forth on *oratio recta* and *oratio obliqua* and offers several styles, including the parody of the legend of Finn MacCool:

I will relate, said Finn. . . . With the eyelids to him stitched to the fringe of his eye-bags, he must be run by Finn's people through the bogs and marsh-swamps of Erin with two odorous prickle-backed hogs ham-tied and asleep in the seat of his hempen drawers. If he sink beneath a peat-swamp or lose a hog, he is not accepted of Finn's people. For five days he must sit on the brow of a cold hill with twelve-pointed stag-antlers hidden in his seat, without food or music or chessmen. . . .

Likewise he must hide beneath a twig, or behind a dried leaf or under a red stone or vanish at full speed into the seat of his hempen drawers without changing his course or abating his pace or angering the men of Erin. Two young fosterlings he must carry under the armpits to his jacket through the whole of Erin and six arm-bearing warriors in his seat together. If he be delivered of a warrior or a blue spear, he is not taken. One hundred head of cattle he must accommodate with wisdom about his person when walking all Erin, the half about his armpits and the half about his trews, his mouth never halting from the discoursing of sweet poetry.

Gradually, the narrative—always alive with interjections, notes of squalor from Dublin realism, and hilarious fantasy—builds up an intrigue: the student is writing a novel about a dull novelist called Trellis who is pillaging other novels. Maimed by the banal treatment they receive from Trellis, the characters get their own back by spreading grotesque yarns about him. In the end Trellis is taken to court, with his characters as judge and jury, in a place remarkably like the bar of a pub. A tram conductor complains that as a character he was made to do a seventy-two-hour week on 'non-pensionable emoluments' and was obliged to speak to his passengers in 'guttersnipe dialect, at all times repugnant to the instincts of a gentleman'. A writer of Wild West tales called Tracy says he was obliged to lend Trellis female characters: 'He explained that technical difficulties relating to ladies' dress had always been an insuperable obstacle to his creation of satisfactory female characters and produced a document purporting to prove that he was reduced on other occasions to utilizing disguised males.' He once lent Trellis a pious girl character who came back 'in a certain condition' six months later. Tracy reinstated the girl in her employment by marrying her to an 'unnecessary person' and got her son a job with a man 'dealing with unknown aspects of the cotton-milling industry'. Some question of a potato-peeler comes up and a judge asks, 'What is a potato-peeler?' The reader notes that the prose of Trellis is a string of clichés.

The absurd trial is, of course, a send-up of the Dublin courts.

Indeed, at every point there are satirical glimpses of Dublin life. If the whole were simple, broad farce, it would soon pall. What transforms it is the comic, if often maddening, influence of Irish pedantry—the comedy of hairsplitting—and O'Brien's ear for the nuances of Dublin talk: above all, for its self-inflating love of formal utterance and insinuation. His humour, as Mr Jones says, depends on the intricacy of its texture. Language is all: he is a native of a country of grammarians, thriving on the perplexities of a mixed culture, and creating, as Joyce did, vulgar or scholarly myths.

To say this is not to underrate O'Brien's superb invention in broad farce—in, say, *The Hard Life*. That book purports to describe the inspired swindles invented by the author's deedy adolescent brother, who makes a start in life by inventing a successful correspondence course in tightrope-walking. He pulls in the money through medical warnings about the dangers of the sport, in a learned pamphlet on giddiness, or Meniere's disease, caused by haemorrhage in 'the equilibristic labyrinth of the ears'. He knows the Irish worship of the grand word:

> The membranous section of the labyrinth consists of two small bags, the saccule and the utricle, and three semi-circular canals which open into it. . . . In the otolith organs the hair-like protuberances are embedded in a gelatinous mess containing calcium carbonate. The purpose of this grandiose apparatus, so far as *homo sapiens* is concerned, is the achievement of remaining in an upright posture, one most desirable in the case of a performer on the high wire.

O'Brien's glee has a double edge—allegorically, Irish life is lived on a 'high wire' or the liberating hope of risk. The boy goes one better by inventing something called Gravid Water, the miracle cure for rheumatism. He achieves a grotesque interview with the Pope. Gravid Water cures rheumatism, but the patient dies of incurable overweight. *The Hard Life* was a late book and, Mr Jones thinks, a step backward—although he does not quite agree that the tale may be an 'exegesis of squalor' or mental sluggishness, common enough in Dublin's stagnant moods. O'Brien's extravagant mock encounters with Joyce (who is heard saying that *Ulysses* was smut written by American academics) and with Keats and Chapman paralytically drunk in a pub after closing time (when the landlord has to declare that the illegal drinkers are all his uncles and nieces) are fun of a journalistic order.

The Dalkey Archives is another matter. Hugh Leonard turned it into the delightful play *When the Saints Go Cycling In*. Here we find the learned De Selby who has scientifically overcome the limitations of time and is able to take his guests under the sea, in a handmade Cousteau-style tank, to meet and gossip scandalously with the Christian saints who deride the Apostles. St Augustine is the arch humbug and is exposed. De Selby is a splendid anti-Prospero who is possessed by the native desire to blow the world to smithereens. O'Brien's narrator is worried by the religious scandal but thinks that the only way to put a stop to De Selby's threat is to have him collaborate on a book like Joyce's epic—say, *Finnegans Wake*—which will so befuddle his mind that he will forget his scheme. Poor O'Brien was near death when he wrote this work and, Mr Jones says, the humour rises far above wit and cleverness and is 'beautiful'. I would have said 'calm and equable'. Another writer has quoted what O'Brien said of Joyce—'With laughs he palliates the sense of doom that is the heritage of the Irish Catholic'—as being a summary of O'Brien's literary and personal tragedy.

The curious theme of death kept at bay by the invention of conceits underlies *The Third Policeman*, the posthumously published version of the early novel that had failed. It seems to have begun as a mock detective story, in which the author is forced to commit an appalling murder by a man who has enslaved him and robbed him of his property. This is a dark and disturbing tale. O'Brien's work is rich in distracting episodes and here we come upon a conceit that seems to point to something obsessive in his inward-turning mind. The conceit reminds one of Borges and of those figures who multiply in a series of reflections in retreating mirrors. In O'Brien the object is a box that contains a box containing boxes, getting infinitely smaller, until they are invisible. It seems that O'Brien put off doom by retreating into a metaphysical solitude. But the scene becomes macabre. Ridiculous policemen arrive. The narrator is arrested and hears a scaffold being built, plank by plank, on which he will be hanged. As an idea, this concentrates an easily distracted mind. Bicycles—another of O'Brien's obsessive groups of objects—confuse the tale, for he cannot resist an idea. But there is no doubt of his laughter and unnerving melancholy.

List of Books

Books referred to

MAX BEERBOHM
Max: Sir Max Beerbohm. By Lord David Cecil, 1964.
A Peep into the Past. Introduction by Rupert Hart-Davis, 1972.
The Lies of Art: Max Beerbohm's Parody and Caricature. By John
Felstiner, 1973.

E. F. BENSON
Make Way for Lucia: The Complete Lucia, 1976.

RIDER HAGGARD
Rider Haggard: his Life and Works. By Morton Cohen, 1960.

RUDYARD KIPLING
The Strange Ride of Rudyard Kipling. By Angus Wilson, 1977.
Kipling: The Glass, the Shadow and the Fire. By Philip Mason,
1975.
Rudyard Kipling: his Life and Work. By Charles Carrington,
1955.

JOSEPH CONRAD
Joseph Conrad: The Three Lives. By Frederick Karl, 1979.

T. E. LAWRENCE
A Prince of our Disorder: The Life of T. E. Lawrence. By John E.
Mack, 1976.

E. M. FORSTER
E. M. Forster: A Life. 2 vols. By P. N. Furbank, 1977 and 1978.

GRAHAM GREENE
The Comedians, 1966.
Graham Greene. By John Atkins, 1966.
Collected Essays, 1969.

EVELYN WAUGH
A Little Learning: An Autobiography, 1964.
Men at Arms, 1962.
Unconditional Surrender, 1961.

ANGUS WILSON
Anglo-Saxon Attitudes, 1956.
No Laughing Matter, 1967.

HENRY GREEN
Blindness, 1926. Re-issued 1977.

HENRY JAMES
A Biography. Vol. 2, *The Conquest of London*. By Leon Edel, 1962.
              Vol. 4, *The Treacherous Years*. By Leon Edel, 1969.
The American Scene. Introduction and notes by Leon Edel, 1969.

EDMUND WILSON
To the Finland Station: a Study in the Writing and Acting of History, 1940. Re-issued 1962.

SAUL BELLOW
Herzog, 1964.
Humboldt's Gift, 1972.

MARY McCARTHY
Birds of America, 1971.

FLANNERY O'CONNOR
Everything That Rises Must Converge, 1966.

SAMUEL PEPYS
Diary. 3 vols. Edited by Robert Latham & William Matthews, 1970.

JONATHAN SWIFT
Jonathan Swift: A Biography. By A. L. Rowse, 1976.

RICHARD BURTON
A Life. By Byron Farwell, 1964.

FREDERICK ROLFE
Frederick Rolfe: Baron Corvo. By Miriam J. Benkowitz, 1977.

LADY MURASAKI
The Tale of Genji. A new translation by Edward G. Seiden-sticker, 1976.
Arthur Waley's translation, 1925-35.

RUTH PRAWER JHABVALA
A New Dominion, 1976.

FLANN O'BRIEN
A Flann O'Brien Reader. Introduction by Stephen Jones, 1977.

About the Author

V. S. PRITCHETT was born in 1900. In addition to being a critic, he is a short-story writer, novelist, biographer, autobiographer, and travel writer. Sir Victor is a foreign honorary member of the American Academy of Arts and Letters and of the Academy of Arts and Sciences. In 1975 he received a knighthood. He lives in London with his wife.

VINTAGE CRITICISM: LITERATURE, MUSIC, AND ART